Post-Modern Terrorism:
Trends, Scenarios, and Future Threats

Edited by Dr. Boaz Ganor

The International Policy Institute for Counter-Terrorism

The Interdisciplinary Center Herzliya

Publishing House

Post-Modern Terrorism:

Trends, Scenarios, and Future Threats

Edited by: **Boaz Ganor**

Cover design: Studio Billet
Language editing: Yael Shahar, Rachel Lieberman
Production: Chaviva Ashkenazi
Typesetting: Rachel Shamir

ISBN 965-7257-06-9

The International Policy Institute for Counter-Terrorism
Herzliya Projects Publishing House Ltd.
The Interdisciplinary Center Herzliya

The International Policy Institute for Counter-Terrorism
Mifalot Herzliya Projects Ltd.
Telephone: 972-9-9527318
Fax: 972-9-9568616

P.O. Box 167
Herzliya 46150, Israel

Printed in Israel — 2005

This book is based on lectures given at ICT's 3rd International Conference, held at the Interdisciplinary Center Herzliya in September 2003.

International Policy Institute for Counter-Terrorism wishes to thank the following organizations and individuals for their sponsorship of The Conference:

    The Embassy of the United States of America in Israel

    IDF Operational Theory Research Institute

    Israel National Security Council, Counter-Terrorism Bureau

    The Rich Foundation

    Israel Foreign Ministry

    BMW

    City of Herzliya

Contents

Preface

From 7-10 September 2003, hundreds of security professionals from all over the world gathered at the International Policy Institute for Counter-Terrorism to participate in the Institute's 3rd International Conference. The topic was *Post-Modern Terrorism: Trends, Scenarios, and Future Threats.*

The conference brought together many of the world's leading security professionals, academic experts, and decision-makers to discuss the nature of terrorism and counter-terrorism in the coming years:

- How will terrorists operate in the future?

- What current and foreseeable conflicts are most likely to spawn terrorism over the next decade?

- What steps should governments take today to protect their citizens from tomorrow's terrorism?

These and other important questions were the focus of three days of intensive discussion by experts from all over the world. This book is a selection of lectures presented at the 3rd International Conference by well-known experts, and provides a timely overview of such topics as terrorism forecasting, the evolution of religiously motivated terrorism, containment of a mega-terror attack, and integrated responses to terrorism. Many other lectures—equally as interesting and as thought provoking—have had to be left out, due to lack of space.

Terrorism, in one form or another, is likely to be with us for the foreseeable future. *Post-Modern Terrorism* provides readers with glimpses of the shape of terrorism in the next decade, according to some of the foremost terrorism scholars and security experts in the world. This is a vision that we ignore at our peril.

Dr. Boaz Ganor
Executive Director

Foreword

HRH Prince El Hassan bin Talal

I am aware I am speaking to an interdisciplinary center and I would like to address from the outset questions that were put to me as a potential participant in this conference and which are before you at this time. Starting with, *"What means may be available to a terrorist in the future?"* You know better than I, that on the subject of the proliferation of weapons of mass destruction and on the stability of the Middle East, a meeting of experts on Middle East regional security and elimination of weapons of mass destruction took place most recently as February 2003 in Airlie House, Virginia.

As a member of the Nuclear Threat Initiative, which is a meaningful contributor to the location of weapons of mass destruction and which is headed by Sam Nunn, former Secretary of Defense and Senator Richard Lugar, I thank them and their group of experts for coordinating projects such as Project Vinca, as described in the Readers Digest of April 2003, that moved enriched uranium to Russia where it would be converted into a form of uranium unsuitable for a nuclear bomb.

Over and above that, since the Evian Conference, I am happy to see that the OCED has taken this process seriously. I am only saddened that actually in terms of the dismantling of weapons of mass destruction and the creation of jobs for those who have worked in this field in the past—turning swords into ploughshares if you will—that it is an NGO that is focusing its efforts in this regard; we expect over $15 billion to be released as an ultimate goal in this current phase.

I refer to weapons of mass destruction because in terms of regional stability in our peace agreement with Israel, we made provisions for—and indeed called for—a "CSC," a Conference of Security and Cooperation in the Middle East. I do believe that the time has come, particularly in the event of a continuation of killings of innocent civilians—of Palestinians, of Israelis, and of the continuing rising toll of terrorist activities—for the legitimacy of a group of reflection, representing the different organizations which have worked with the subject of crisis avoidance and promoting policies, rather than acting on an ad hoc basis and in direct response to current security issues. It would recognize that terrorism is a basic security issue, in a swath of countries which include Arab countries, non-Arab countries such as Israel, and of course Iran, Turkey, Pakistan and possibly to the borders of India.

We are accustomed all over the world, in the context of post-modernist terror, to living under an oligarchy of one kind or another, a form of government by a small group of people. The parallel economy of terror is also a form of a government by a small unelected group of people. But I might also add that we are now entering a phase of rule by, if you'll forgive me, an oil-igarchy, that is to say, in the oil producing region in this part of the world, the small group of people who control the movement and supply of the world's energy resources, in both the parallel economic and social systems. Let me be quite frank, one of the causes of terrorism is the breakdown of governance at the popular level. I do feel that this issue needs a code of conduct which makes incremental progress where it can.

We have gone as far as we can on the question of weapons of mass destruction and the question of basic regional security, or basic regional commons if you will. We talk about global commons and we talk about regional commons. Let us make it clear that one of the regional commons in the Euro-Med/Nato-Med region is the focus on the preventative measures against incoming migrants from the Asian or African countries. I am only sorry that preventative measures were not taken when Shimon Peres and I called for them in Casablanca back in 1994. We called for an investment of $35 billion to encourage the will of potential migrants to stay. Sadly, the Homeland Security bill was $35 billion, which is the equivalent of what would have been spent over ten years to prevent the movement of people who can turn unfortunately to the Mafios, in the Balkans, in Afghanistan and elsewhere, for ready money.

I would like to suggest that we should be considering in this conference, under the rubric of what means may be available to terrorists in the future, not only the accounting for illegal sources of funding, but also the fact that the parallel grey economy has in fact destabilized the legitimate economy of these countries.

Your country and ours are members of aspirants, rather, to membership of the European Community; I signed an agreement in 1974 with Syria and Egypt. But unfortunately we do not represent a core group of a critical mass recognized by the European Community. They allocate names to us; we *are Mashreq countries*, I am an Asian, you as an Israeli, are European. When you wish to be, you are a Middle Easterner. I am not being presumptuous, but I am just referring to United Nations terminologies. I think the time has come to recognize the importance of the Eastern Mediterranean and the Black Sea region, both as the European rim of Asia and as the Asian rim of Europe. Because if we talk about throughput, not only of oil from the Russian Confederation across Europe, now possibly marginalizing some of the transit countries such as Germany, we should also talk in terms of the throughput of illegal matter and we know very well what the Danube represented in terms of the attempts at smuggling narcotics during the Balkan crisis. I recall travelling with an Israeli Minister—Yossi Sarid—at the time, when we travelled with the optimistic slogan, "Peace in the Middle East, Peace to the Balkans" in 1995. How far we are now from that, and how impertinent possibly we were in carrying this slogan. In the broader conversations over coalitions—we have heard a lot about the coalition of the willing—I'd like to say something about the coalition of the coherent, and I hope that this coherence can be developed in the understanding of the common threats that we face.

As for the Peace Process I just want to say that when identifying your second question, *How will current trends in religion and culture influence the future of terrorism?* I thank you for emphasizing the importance of religion and culture. But I would like to say that the Barcelona baskets and the Helsinki Process baskets, usually emphasize security, politics and economy, with culture as an after-thought. Now for me, culture is security and multiple identity is security, pluralism is security and democracy cannot be built without the respect for the other, whether he be Arab, Christian, Muslim or Jew.

I would like to point out that part of the sadness that I feel over the building of the wall today around Jerusalem is that it isolates liberal Jews from liberal Arabs. Actually, the human rights movement in Israel has done some outstanding work but I hope that this separation and this isolation will not mean that the majority of the "sane," if I can put it that way—and I still believe that there is a majority of the sane that yearns for peace—can hold the necessary exchanges in emphasizing soft security and human security. There is too much emphasis on hard security, that is to say police action and military action, and I go back to the fact that you are an inter-disciplinary center and say that particularly since 9/11 the battle has been one of a "war on terror." So, as my late friends Yehudi Menuhin and Walter Sisulu in South Africa used to say, "Isn't it about time that we stopped working against something and started working for a mobilization of something positive?" Here I think the mobilization should be of the majority of the sane.

I was reading Judah Magnes the other day, and I find that the criticism within Israel of the acts of resistance, the killings that took place during the formative years of the movements that led to the creation of the State of Israel and to its independence, were described as, "dissenting movements," that is to say dissenting from the spirit of the creation of the State of Israel. I would like to refer quite clearly to the term, "Islamist;" and as a Hashemite and descendent from the House of the Prophet (PBUH), I don't have to describe myself as an "Islamist." I am a Muslim. But when it comes to the question of terror, I think that this branding of "terrorist" with Islam is unfortunately a by-product of the end of the Cold War and the collapse of the Berlin Wall. A new enemy had to be sought. It used to be "reds under the bed," today it is "greens under the bed" and I am not referring to our conservationist friends. I am referring to Muslims. Of course there are other groupings which are listed on terrorist organizations' lists, including Basques, including various Latin American groupings, including various Irish groupings, but nobody refers to them as "Christianist terrorists." In fact in Northern Ireland I received a degree in a University from a Jewish Chancellor in a non-denominational university and as a Muslim recipient I said, "Why is it that you refer to Islamist terror? Why not refer to Christianist terror?" I think they got my point.

I do think that in terms of the cultural trends in the Middle East region, that it is important to bear in mind that a humanitarian Marshall Plan is required with a focus on poverty alleviation. I noticed that in a recent edition of *Ha'aretz* a poll was held on the Israeli quality of life. As quoted by *Ha'aretz*, 83%, were very satisfied with their life. Now I am not envying them that satisfaction, but I do want to say that when one looks at Iraq today, oil-rich Iraq, the per capita is less than $600, so the disparity means that those organizations that have ready money—it is true that Saddam Hussein according to Mr. Bremer is travelling around with two lorry loads of money behind him—are there to offer immediate intervention, possibly mobilizing suicide bombings and the like, as abominable as they are, and as we all deplore them. To emphasize the importance of culture, I do think that if a group of reflection ever comes to pass it should be inter-disciplinary and it should attend to the subject of a close look at what the Europeans have achieved in terms of historical learning by analogy, that is to say revisiting your own text, history and heritage and revisiting that of the other. I think that changing attitudes and changing mindsets can only be achieved in this context.

As for the outstanding question of cultural and religious trends, I want to make it very clear that culture is an after-thought. I remember Jim Woolsey saying, "Going into Iraq without sensitivity for local culture would be like the 7th cavalry going into Indian territory without interpreters." Your own Chief of Defense Staff said, "With all due respect to the American military, that in such a situation a third-rate Iraqi policeman is better than a first-rate American." Now this is not a criticism of the training of the American soldier, but a matter of common sense; the ability to circulate, to know the local atmosphere is so important, that I think this is the quality that needs to be revisited in terms of: a stand-by force, an international army of soldiers and of policemen ready to participate but fully aware of the cultural background of the situation that they are getting themselves into. In that sense I think that such arrangements would truly emphasize the importance, not of a unipolar world or multipolar world but of a multilateral world. I noticed Secretary Rumsfeld yesterday asking the press, "How many nationalities do we have?" They told him, "29" and he said, "Well we need more". With all due respect, I would suggest that we need more qualitative participation; it is very difficult to take a fighting soldier, whether in the Palestinian Territories as you know better than I, or in Iraq, or in Afghanistan or in Yugoslavia and turn him or her into a local pastoral leader, contacting local leaders, building civil society, building the participation of ordinary men and women under that famous and reverberating American slogan 'We, the people'.

Culturally, there has been too much building from the top down, emphasizing the trickle-down effect. The largesse of totalitarian regimes has not worked; the time has now come to start building from the bottom up. I think we have passed through three phases of traditional regimes, the neo-nationalist regimes from Nasser through Saddam Hussein—I notice with some interest, some concern, that Libya is paying huge sums of money to reinstate itself internationally after the death of innocents in the crash of two international aircraft in 'incidents', and I wonder whether this is a trend. Is it possible for countries to call the measure of the international community? I would rather suggest that the conference takes seriously into account the presentation made to the General Assembly of the United Nations, of a proposal for the implementation of compliance in the field of international humanitarian and human rights law[1]. Let me make it very clear that it should apply to both state and non-state actors. "Because hiding behind one excuse or another", if I may quote, "governments tend to violate international humanitarian and human rights law and by-pass the universally accepted norms and principles and thus cause a lot of suffering. In such a situation international reprimands or pressures for compliance are often ignored". I would also like to make it very clear that the Swedish Government proposal to formulate a set of fundamental standards of humanity on the basis of international law and human rights is something I would love to hear Mr. Bush speaking about in the United Nations in a few days time. Working for something again; we have so many concessions with the law of war that we do not have a law of peace, and I think that in the war on terror, the war on our infinite capacity to destroy each other

---

1 Project Proposal to Problems of Implementation and Compliance in the Field of International Humanitarian and Human Rights Law, Presented by The United Nations Office for Coordination of Humanitrian Affairs (OCHA) and The Independent Bureau for Humanitarian Issues (IBHI), June 2000.

many times over, in the war on poverty and hunger—let's remember the carrot as well as the stick. The time has come for talking about extra-territorial, extra-national priorities in this region, not only talking about, but actually getting into the creation of a community of water and energy, just like Europe started with coal and steel, which is after all an extra-national priority. In terms of culture and education, talking once again of another extra-national priority, and that is educating our young and involving our young in these humanitarian and human rights norms.

I want to summarize in terms of trends by saying that, clearly, terrorist organizations have been forced underground but by no means eliminated. I don't know how many of them are being listed in the new lists of terrorist organizations and if such lists actually address the issue, because as you know they multiply with a variety of names, as odious as they are. I think they will continue to search for gaps in security, they will continue the consideration of possible targets with an impact on populations such as infrastructure and also they will continue thinking of military targets. I ask myself, with a spread of 26 American bases from Iran to China, whether this emphasis is going to be on a strategic perception of stabilizing the region, or whether it is also going to be on the subject of scenarios and future threats, and in that I would like to add infrastructures; especially targets that would cause panic and fear, targets of opportunity where they have active operational cells, targets which would aim to cause continuous fear in population.

Labeling your enemy a terrorist is naming your opposition a terrorist and this is not a solution in itself. I think that no single country can solve the issue of global security alone, and the time really is right for a moral authority and legitimacy of foreign policy action that should derive from an agreed multilateral, international order. So I hope to hear from President Bush, in this speech, or in a future statement, an emphasis on working for an ethic of human solidarity and for an international humanitarian order. I do not believe that the question of security, with all due respect to the military, should be left to the military alone, and I once again emphasize the importance of people's participation in identifying their responsibilities. The ceiling to freedom as I have said—I would love to hold a meeting with all the Arab Ministers of the

Interior to ask them what the ceiling to freedom is—is responsibility. As to what steps governments should take to protect their citizens from terrorists, the greater the citizen is empowered, the more he is aware of his relevance and the better it is. In Pakistan and in India after 9/11 I recall, the export of textiles was forbidden and I want to say that at least in one project of which I am familiar in Southern Pakistan, 400,000 families were thrown into the lap of alternative sources of funding. As I said to our American friends, these people don't need weapons they need food and they need employment.

As for your last question, *What can be done to predict future terrorist attacks?*, I think the closer we come to each other, the more we maintain human contact, the more we emphasize policy rather than politics—which makes us look individually good for the moment with our respective constituents, and policies which look at the ten-year trends—the more likely it is that we can make a change. But in the words of the Psychoanalysis, by Jean-Marie La Cannes and his translation of Sigmund Freud, "If you want to change something, then you need clarity about what it is we want to change".

Shalom.

International Terrorism Trends

The Feasibility of Post-Modern Terrorism

Dr. Boaz Ganor

Executive Director, International Policy Institute for Counter-Terrorism, Israel

While some may argue that non-conventional terrorism is only a matter of time—and not much time, at that—others insist that it is premature to worry about such "alarmist" scenarios. After all, they reason, the sarin gas attack perpetrated by Aum Shirinkyo ("Supreme Truth") cult in the Tokyo subway actually proved that even if a terror organization is capable of acquiring non-conventional means, it still lacks the practical capability to perpetrate the attack due to the deficiency of effective dispersal means. Thus, these theorists argue that though the threat is extremely grave, the prospects of perpetration are minimal.

In order to determine which of these two schools of thought is right, it would be helpful to classify the types of possible non-conventional attacks. While it is customary to differentiate between attacks according to which substance is used—chemical, biological, nuclear, or radiological—one can also classify attacks by the intended result. Thus, attacks using non-conventional means can be "limited" or "unlimited" in nature.

A "limited" non-conventional attack differs from the usual terrorist bombing only in the means used. As in the case of a conventional attack, the limited non-conventional attack aims to cause multiple casualties at the site of the attack or in its immediate vicinity. And like a conventional terror attack, this type of terror attack attempts to draw media and public attention to the messages and demands of the terror organization by inflicting extensive casualties and spreading public anxiety—the ultimate goal being to influence political processes of the target population.

A limited non-conventional terror attack could be carried out by dispersing a chemical substance in an enclosed space, by contaminating food and water sources, or by using explosives to disperse a radiological agent at a selected location. Another example of a limited non-conventional attack would be a destructive assault on a facility containing dangerous substances, such as a military or industrial facility. In all of these examples, the damage is of limited scope, albeit potentially far more serious than a non-conventional attack on the same target. In general, the majority of chemical attacks would be "limited" in scope (see diagram).

Figure 1: Types of Non-Conventional Terrorism

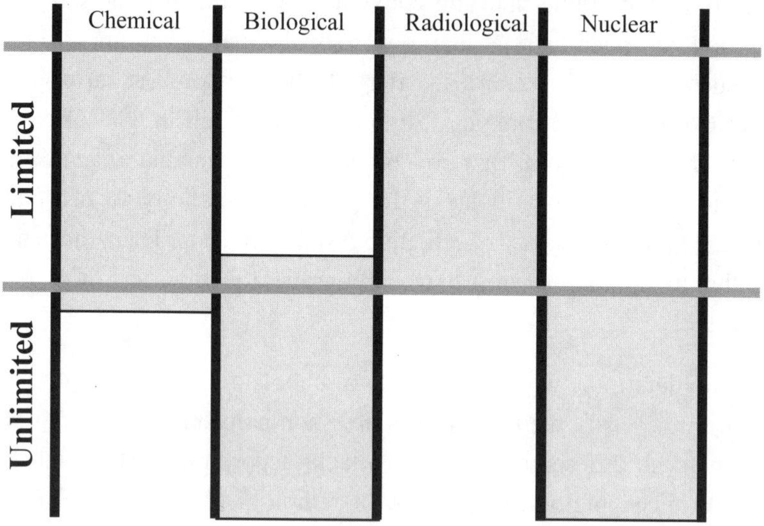

Figure 1: Chemical attacks are mostly "limited" in scope, while biological attacks are mostly "unlimited" with a few exceptions such as Anthrax and other non-contagious agents. Nuclear attacks are always "unlimited" due to their severe ecological impact, while radiological attacks are always "limited" in scope.

In contrast to "limited" attacks, "unlimited" attacks are not meant merely to incur damage and carnage in a specific and focused public area. Rather, they are designated to destroy or contaminate large areas (a town, village, city, a specific geographical area, etc.). The conceptual basis for these two categories of attacks differs: While tactical, or limited, non-conventional terror is designated to serve as leverage to alter a political reality through the use of intimidation, unlimited non-conventional terror strives to change the political reality itself *de facto* by annihilating large populations, contaminating extensive geographical regions, etc. This type of attack may also have severe psychological impact on public morale—an impact that may completely undermine the population's confidence in government institutions and their values. Yet even without this effect, the unlimited non-conventional attack causes grave and prolonged damage to the area under attack, thus immediately affecting reality.

For unlimited non-conventional terror attacks, terror organizations will primarily prefer nuclear or biological weapons, followed by some types of chemical weapons; radiological substances are generally unsuited to this type of attack. An unlimited non-conventional attack could involve the effective dispersal of hazardous substances, or the long-term contamination of water sources or reservoirs, and national or regional food stocks through the use of chemical and/or biological substances. Some biological agents are especially suited for such an attack, since they can spread on their own after their initial dispersal and are thus "unlimited" by their nature. An attacker might choose to attack a facility containing non-conventional substances in a way that will ensure the spreading of the contamination beyond the immediate vicinity. This form of attack exceeds the boundaries of a limited threat, becoming an "extreme" threat when the attack is directed against nuclear facilities or facilities containing hazardous biological substances located in proximity to densely populated areas.

The classification of non-conventional terror attacks into limited attacks and unlimited attacks can go a long way toward resolving the dispute regarding the likelihood that non-conventional terror attacks will be perpetrated in the foreseeable future. More precisely, while it would be accurate to say that "limited" non-conventional terror attacks are within the range of many organizations, the use of "unlimited" non-conventional terrorism is still a long way off. At the same time, even limited non-conventional attacks may not be the modus operandi of choice for most terrorist organizations.

To understand why, let us examine the factors that might influence a terrorist organization's use of non-conventional terrorism. An organization might be influenced by any of the following factors:

1. **Unlimited non-conventional attacks require a change in mindset –** While limited non-conventional attacks might be considered "raising the ante" while not necessarily breaking "the rules of the game,"

unlimited non-conventional attacks would necessitate a complete rethinking of the terror organization's operational strategy.

2. **The fear of punitive measures** – It stands to reason that the response to a limited non-conventional attack will be less severe and more contained than the retaliation in the aftermath of a non-conventional terror attack causing the deaths of thousands of people and the contamination of extensive geographical areas.

3. **The fear of harming a supportive population** – Many terror organizations rely on the assistance of a supportive population or claim to represent such a population; the more severe type of non-conventional attack could pose a danger to the health and lives of the supportive population—particularly in the event of an unlimited non-conventional attack.

4. **Moral and ethical considerations** – Some of the organizations attempt to rationalize their attacks with excuses that they believe justify harming civilians; however these rationalization attempts attest to the existence of an ethical dilemma. The perpetration of unlimited non-conventional attacks would make it much more difficult to persuade both internal and external entities of the justification for using such means than would be the case for carrying out a limited non-conventional attack.

If, in addition to all of these points, one takes into consideration how difficult it is to obtain non-conventional substances, as well as effective means of dispersal, we can conclude that the perpetration of a limited non-conventional terror attack is much more likely than the perpetration of an unlimited non-conventional attack.

One of the main questions that must therefore be considered is: Which organizations are most likely to use non-conventional means? Or in other words, what are the indicators that may point to the possibility that a terror organization will indeed perpetrate non-conventional terror?

Only when an organization has both the operational capability and the motivation to perpetrate a particular type of attack will the attack come to pass. With regard to a non-conventional terror attack, the motivation factor takes on supreme importance, both because of the relative difficulty to acquire the necessary capabilities, and due to the grave consequences that may result from the attack and boomerang back upon the organization itself.

The motivation to perpetrate non-conventional terror attacks can be divided into incentive stemming from rational motives and incentive stemming from irrational motives.

Motivation stemming from a rational motive – "rational" from the aspect of evaluation and weighing cost/benefit considerations prior to perpetrating the attack). Possible motivating factors may include acquiescence to the request of a sponsor state or a state that operates the terror organization, a desire to escalate the conflict, a desire to change reality, emulation and competition, or the belief that "there is no other alternative."

- **Acquiescence to the request of a sponsor state or a state that operates the terror organization** – In this case, the motivation to perpetrate the attack is forced upon the organization by the supporting and sponsoring state, or the organization willingly serves as a means to perpetrate the attack and the latter is basically designated to serve the needs and interests of that state. In this event, the state itself may supply the organization with the required means prior to the attack.

- **The aspiration to escalate the struggle** – One of the basic motives that a terror organization may have to start perpetrating non-conventional terror attacks is the desire to escalate the struggle against the state. This incentive may stem from two main sources: The first—as the result of successful counter-terror activity conducted by the state against the organization which inflicted serious damage upon the latter and significantly increased the thirst for revenge among its activists and leadership, and the second—due to a feeling in the organization that the "conventional" means have been fully tapped, and they no longer have the power to evoke the media coverage and public attention that they did in the past; thus, they no longer have impact on the political arena and are unable to bring about the desired change that the organization aspires to achieve. In these circumstances, the terror organizations may decide that the time has come to perpetrate spectacular attacks with multiple fatalities, which break the game rules known to date and force the media and public opinion to pay attention to the terrorists' demands. The non-conventional terror weapon is the most suitable means for this type of task.

- **The aspiration to change reality** – Terror organizations generally aspire to influence approaches and political processes in order to alter a social, economic, or political order. Terror attacks serve the organization as a tool to convey messages in a violent manner, frighten the public, place issues on the internal and global public agenda, and exert pressure on decision makers to cave in to the terror organizations' demands. A non-conventional terror attack may be perpetrated by a terror organization not only in order to escalate the struggle and raise the price that the state is forced to pay due to its refusal to change the existing order, but also as a result of the organization's desire to independently alter the political reality by annihilating a significant number of people, entire communities, and/or contaminating large areas, thereby preventing their use. These types of motivations may grow against the background of religious, national or ethnic conflict.

- **Emulation and competition** – The use of non-conventional terror by a given terror organization, and the media coverage following in the wake of this attack may motivate another terrorist organization to perpetrate non-conventional terror in order to emulate or compete with other organizations. From this aspect, the adoption of non-conventional activity by one organization may be perceived as the initial shattering of the taboo, which will enable other organizations to take this course. (This development did not occur in the aftermath of the attacks perpetrated by the Aum Shirinkyo ("Supreme Truth") cult in Tokyo—this may be due to the isolation of Japanese society vis-à-vis other societies worldwide and the relative failure of these attacks to cause multiple deaths at the attack site.) It is important to stress in this connection that by the same token, the failure of terror organizations to perpetrate non-conventional terror attacks in addition to the anticipated harsh retaliation of the attacked states and the international community may serve as a restraining or mitigating factor when it comes to the organization's motivation to initiate this type of attack.

- **Access to non-conventional substances** – This variable is ostensibly related to the operational capability area rather than the motivational aspect. However, it is important to take into account that when a terror organization is given the opportunity to obtain non-conventional means and acquire the necessary knowledge to carry out this type of attack, even if the organization had no original attention to utilize these means, the issue will then be placed on the internal agenda and considered by decision makers within the organization. From this aspect, access to these substances may serve to spur the organization's motivation to adopt non-conventional activities.

- **A feeling that "there is no other alternative"** – This refers to organizations that are in a state of decline and are at risk of becoming extinct. Whether due to the removal of external support, diminished support among its population of origin, or effective counter-actions that inflicted severe damage on the organization (arrest/elimination of the organization's leadership, eradication of most of its economic and operational infrastructure, etc.). In this regard it is noteworthy that the leader's perception of the organization's state, as well as the subjective sensation of deterioration and fear of extinction, are more significant than the organization's actual state. Thus, the organization's leadership may opt for desperate measures in the form of non-conventional means even when the danger of extinction does not really exist.

Motivation stemming from an irrational motive – Alongside motives stemming from rational incentive, there may be others in which cost/benefit considerations or the price to be paid by the perpetrating organization are not taken into account. In this case, the set of considerations that concerns the terror organization is totally different and draws upon the authority of some power outside the usual socio-political arena—a divine power or faith in a prophet or apocalyptic ideology.

- **Religious faith in a divine decree** – The belief that the use of non-conventional weapons fulfills a divine decree necessitating the removal of evil from the world by eradicating whole communities and even destroying all human life. This faith is based on the assumption that the world has deviated from the righteous path and there is no alternative but to rebuild it after wiping out humanity. With the exception of a group of believers and the enlightened few who are members of the organization.

- **Faith in the "end of days" ideology** – Belief in the need for structural, demographic, or religious and ideological change on a certain date, which holds symbolic-religious meaning for the group. This belief is usually the result of perpetual brainwashing among groups and societies that revolve around a charismatic leader—a religious prophet, a preacher or a spiritual mentor. This type of organization generally takes the form of a cult and is characterized by the eradication of independent will and identity through subjugation to the wishes and path set by the leader, to the extent of being willing to commit suicide or kill on his behalf.

In light of everything stated above, the question arises: Is it possible to identify various characteristics that may enable prediction of the prospect that an organization might be inclined to use non-conventional attacks?

The characteristics of a particular terror organization have a direct or indirect impact on the organization's motivation and its operational capability to perpetrate non-conventional terror attacks. Variables that may serve as predictors for the organization's motivation to perpetrate non-conventional attacks include:

1. **Characteristics of previous attacks** – One must study the main types of attacks perpetrated by an organization whilst placing special emphasis on their degree of lethality and indiscrimination. Thus, it is important to differentiate between "personal" terror attacks directed at a specific person and "guerilla" attacks focused directly and selectively upon military targets and facilities on the one hand, and indiscriminate "lethal attacks" headed by "suicide attacks" (whose realization depends completely upon the death of the perpetrator himself) on the other.

2. **The current state of achievements** – This variable refers to the organization's level of achievements and failures both from the aspect of ongoing terror activity—(its success in perpetrating planned attacks), and from the aspect of the organization's strategic goals its— ability to garner achievements on the international and local scale, and to realize its strategic interests and objectives. From this point of view, it stands to reason that an organization experiencing continuous successes (success in perpetrating attacks that cause multiple deaths and generate media impact, and success in realizing political goals and objectives) will not consider modifying its attack policy and will not have a need for non-conventional attacks. On the other hand, an organization suffering from a series of tactical failures, resulting in an inability to attract the limelight of the media and public and failure to promote its objectives using conventional methods, may consider using non-conventional means in order to end the sequence of failures.

3. **Goals** – One of the most cardinal predictors vis-à-vis the organization's motivation to perpetrate non-conventional attacks is the goals that serve as the foundation for the organization's policies and for which it was established. In this framework one must distinguish between four categories of goals and objectives:

    ▪ **Religious goals** – Goals designated to disseminate religious belief, vanquish another religion, convert the population's religion, fulfill God's wishes and wage a Holy War. Goals stemming from a religious authority which aim to achieve religious objectives through the preference of one religion over another may constitute the motive for an all out war— (wars that only end when one group subjugates the will of another or in even graver circumstances, when one group is obliterated). The use of non-conventional means may well aid the terror organization in achieving these goals.

    ▪ **Nationalist-racist goals** – These are goals designated to eliminate a certain group of people whether through physical purging, deprivation of its political power, subjugation, or any other means. In these cases, the organizations act against specific ethnic groups while espousing an ideological-racist platform that discriminates between populations on the basis of race, religion or nationality. When the demographic distribution correlates directly with the geographical distribution within a given area there is a danger that the terror organization will be tempted to use non-conventional means in order to inflict severe damage on or even eliminate the rival population.

- **Social goals** – Goals designated to alter an existing social order either through political revolution and the ousting of a government or stemming from an anarchist worldview. From this angle, the danger of using non-conventional means mainly exists in organizations that espouse an anarchist worldview. They are not necessarily interested in seizing the reins of government or creating a new and more just world order, but rather seek the destruction of the existing world order for its own sake.

- **National goals** – This context includes goals designed to change the existing delineation of state boundaries while annexing areas of other states or relinquishing territories in favor of neighboring countries. These goals are also related to self-determination and national liberation in the framework of which a group strives to break away from the state and establish an independent political entity. These goals may trigger severe rivalry between the majority and minority groups in the state, but as long as the minority group is intermingled with the majority group, the use of non-conventional means (in unlimited attacks aimed at annihilating groups and neutralizing extensive areas) may endanger the lives of the population that supports the terror organization and the disputed territory, thus constituting a factor that limits the organization's ability to perpetrate this type of attack.

4. **Threats and statements** – One of the possible indications to gauge a terror organization's motivation to perpetrate non-conventional terror attacks is the existence or non-existence of statements and direct or indirect threats issued by the heads of the terror organization and its senior activists in this regard. From this aspect, a series of statements as well as threats to utilize these means may indicate the organization's intentions or at least point to internal discussions taking place inside the organization regarding the non-conventional issue. (It is noteworthy that statements made by organization activists stressing the non-conventional capabilities of a rival state may also serve as an indication of special awareness vis-à-vis the non-conventional issue among the organization's activists.)

5. **Organization leadership** – The organization's structure and leadership may affect its inclination to use non-conventional means. From this point of view, the more decentralized and democratic the leadership, the greater the reason to assume that there is less chance of raising the required consensus to deviate from accepted norms and start using unlimited non-conventional means. In contrast, in the event that the leadership is more centralized and organizational policy is set by one man—a charismatic leader standing at the head of the organization—then this decision may be taken more easily.

6. **The decision-making process within the organization** – As stated above, it is possible to divide the decision-making processes in a terror organization into two categories—a rational process and an irrational process. An organization adopting irrational decision-making processes that are not based on cost/benefit considerations will be insensitive to the possible consequences of the perpetration of non-conventional attacks or to the price that it may be forced to pay for perpetrating these attacks. For this reason, the irrational decision-making process must be regarded as one of the predictors for the use of non-conventional means.

7. **The fear of impending extinction** – As stated above, a terror organization may shift in the direction of non-conventional means in its attacks when it (justifiably or unjustifiably) feels threatened and

in danger of extinction. In this case, the organization may use non-conventional terror as a final act of desperation in an attempt to leave its mark and impact on the world a short time before its final demise.

However, as noted earlier, motivation on the part of a terror organization to perpetrate non-conventional attacks is not sufficient. A precondition for the occurrence of this sort of attack is the existence of the organization's operational ability to perpetrate it. This capability includes the possession of non-conventional materials and/or the substances necessary for their production, the technological knowledge to process these substances into effective combat means, the technological infrastructure necessary for the implementation of the processing, or alternatively the procurement of preprocessed non-conventional combat substances. (Here it is necessary to distinguish between non-conventional substances that may be used for the purposes of a limited lethal attack in which the incurred damage does not greatly exceed the anticipated damage caused by conventional attacks on the one hand, and the combat means necessary for the perpetration of an unlimited non-conventional attack which may cause the annihilation of a wide population and thousands of casualties, as well as extensive environmental contamination, on the other.)

Among the most important predictors for the assessment of the operational capability of a terror organization to perpetrate unlimited non-conventional terror attacks are the following issues:

1. **The organization's economic status** – The organization's economic status may affect its ability to procure raw materials, the finished substances, the technological knowledge, and technological infrastructure necessary for the preparation and perpetration of unlimited non-conventional attacks. All of these aspects generally require significant economic resources that are not available to every organization. Therefore, an adequate economic infrastructure must be regarded as one of the indications of the possibility to create operational capabilities.

2. **State support** – Aid received from various states may preclude the terror organization's need for independent economic and technological resources. Thus, the fact that an organization is supported by a state

that sponsors terror which provides it with financing, or may in fact possess non-conventional capabilities and have the capacity to hand over finished non-conventional substances, all constitute predictors regarding the possibility that the organization will make use of non-conventional means in unlimited attacks. On the other hand, it is important to consider that the state's sponsorship of the terror organization will constitute a restraining factor vis-à-vis the organization's motivation to perpetrate unlimited non-conventional terror due to that country's unwillingness to be accused of any involvement in that type of attack.

3. **Scientific and technological know-how and experience** – One of the most important indicators for gauging the terror organization's operational capability to use non-conventional terror is the existence or non-existence of relevant technological and scientific know-how and experience. Here it is important to take into account that an organization possessing human resources with technological know-how and experience in the nuclear, chemical and biological fields may give more serious consideration to the possibility of using unlimited non-conventional terror to achieve its goals than an organization that lacks experience and know-how in this area.

4. **Access to non-conventional substances and raw materials** – The organization's access to the non-conventional substances themselves and/or to the raw substances unequivocally indicates its ability to carry out this type of terror attack. An analysis of the organization's access to these substances may therefore serve as a predictor vis-à-vis the possibility that the organization will at some time use them in an attack.

In summary, in the course of any attempt to predict which terror organization may use unlimited non-conventional terror, the focus should be placed on the above-mentioned criteria and the fulfillment of each of these conditions in the examined organization. The more indications that apply to the organization, so the prospect becomes greater that it will use non-conventional means. Nevertheless, even in the event that a certain organization meets all of the accumulative preconditions, there is no certainty that it will decide to perpetrate a non-conventional attack. This decision would also depend on internal political circumstances inside the organization, the inter-organizational arena, the local arena (encompassing the attacked country and the terror organization), the organization's relationships with the sponsoring states, and the existing situation in the international arena. Despite this stipulation, it is probable that the criteria and predictors specified above may be helpful when endeavoring to identify organizations with the potential to utilize non-conventional means in the future. Based on these overall indications, the question arises: Is it possible to focus on some of these predictors in order to examine the possibility that a terror organization will attempt to perpetrate a "limited attack" using non-conventional means, in comparison to the possibility that it will decide to carry out an "unlimited non-conventional attack" with these means?

Among the characteristics that may serve as major predictors regarding the motivation of a terror organization to perpetrate a non-conventional "limited attack," the following points must be noted:

- **Characteristics of previous attacks** – In this framework, one must investigate whether the organization has previous experience and specialization in conducting mega attacks using standard and/ or improvised explosives. From this point of view, the transition from perpetrating mega attacks by detonating explosive devices to perpetrating the same type of attack through the use of non-conventional means (chemical or radiological) may yield similar results from the aspect of the extent of the damage and the number of casualties, and may therefore be considered by the terror organizations as a change in method and perhaps even a raising of the ante, but not "crossing the Rubicon."

- **The organization's current state of achievements** – It is important to take into consideration that an organization that was unsuccessful in its conventional activity (i.e., it did not achieve the desired goals and failed to attract the anticipated media coverage) despite the fact that the organization sought to intensify the activity by choosing severe types of attacks (multiple deaths and mass destruction, suicide), or targeting sensitive state facilities (crowded civilian centers, sensitive military areas, etc.), may decide as a last resort to escalate its activity and ensure the obtainment of the desired media coverage and public limelight by using non-conventional means to perpetrate "limited attacks."

- **Past threats and statements** – This predictor may indicate the organization's existing state of mind and enable examination of the possible use of non-conventional means for "limited attacks."

Regarding central indications pointing to the operational capability of a terror organization to perpetrate "limited non-conventional terror," the following points must be noted:

- **Previous technological know-how and experience** – The presence of activists with a suitable technological background and the expertise of organization members in preparing "conventional" explosive devices with chemical substances may serve as indications of the possibility that the organization could use this knowledge and expertise to graduate from the use of chemical substances for explosive devices to the utilization of identical or similar substances for contamination, asphyxiation, etc. in a non-conventional format.

- **Access to raw materials** – A terror organization's access to raw materials which can serve for the preparation of non-conventional means enabling "limited attacks" (though without sophisticated dispersal means), may constitute an additional indication that a terror organization will attempt to carry out this type of attack.

Among the characteristics that may serve as main indicators vis-à-vis the possible motivation of a terror organization to perpetrate an "unlimited attack," the following points must be noted:

- **Characteristics of previous attacks** – Mainly, previous experience in perpetrating suicide attacks and mega attacks. This is based on the assumption that in many cases the scenarios of unlimited non-conventional attacks will necessitate the suicide of the perpetrator and may even cause the deaths of many of the organization's activists.

- **Leadership** – Crucial importance must be attributed to the characteristics of the organization's leadership when attempting to evaluate the possibility of perpetrating these types of attacks. Here it stands to reason that a decision to annihilate an entire community or contaminate extensive geographical areas will be more easily made by a strong centralized and charismatic leadership based on a single figure or a small number of charismatic individuals led by a messianic figure or religious source of authority.

- **The decision-making process** – Due to the radical implications of "unlimited non-conventional attacks" and because of the extensive (and perhaps even existential) damage that may be inflicted upon an organization perpetrating this type of attack, it would seem that the decision to perpetrate this attack will sometimes be based on irrational decision making (without taking cost/benefit considerations into account).

- **The fear of impending extinction** – One of the possible indicators pointing to an attempt by a terror organization to perpetrate strategic non-conventional attacks using non-conventional means is the fear of the leadership and activists that the organization is on the verge of extinction. This fear may tip the scales when considering whether to perpetrate this type of attack (based on the assumption that they possess the capability to do so).

- **Goals** – Racist goals may also serve as indication of the terror organization's motivation to annihilate populations and whole communities via scenarios of unlimited non-conventional attacks.

With regard to key predictors that indicate the terror organization's motivation and operational ability to perpetrate non-conventional attacks, based on the post-9/11 trends of international terrorism, one can conclude that the likelihood of the occurrence of limited non-conventional attacks is much greater than that of unlimited attacks. This is especially true when the characteristics of radical Islamic terrorism—most of which fit the above model—are taken into account.

Modern Terrorism Trends: Reevaluation after 9/11

Dr. Bruce Hoffman

Rand Corporation, Washington, USA

Let me just say a few words about the genesis of this lecture. It was originally conceived nearly six months ago, in March and April of 2003, and it was written specifically in response to what I thought were some overly optimistic assessments about Al Qaida's future and longevity being offered at the time, as well as about the progress of the war against terrorism. For example, on the front page of the Washington Post on Sunday March 16th, there appeared what I considered a remarkable article, that it in essence declared that the war on terrorism was over; that we are finished fighting this war. Astonishingly, a month later (shortly after the conquest of Baghdad), a similar article appeared on the front page of the Washington Times. It struck me that there was a fundamental misunderstanding about Al Qaida and about the dimensions of the problems that we face.

I will focus very briefly on three broad themes. Firstly—and I think that you have to be very suspicious of any terrorism specialist who says anything different—right now we are in the midst of an enormous period of change and transition, and we do not know how it is going to develop. That's why the subject of this conference, post-modern terrorism, is both so timely and so relevant to the problems we face. Because I think terrorism is changing and therefore our understanding of terrorism is shifting.

I think this is very clearly demonstrated in some of the events that we have witnessed in recent months. Certainly, we have scored tremendous successes in the war against terrorism. We have deprived Al Qaida of its operational bases in Afghanistan; we have crushed its operational infrastructure in that country and we have scattered Al Qaida. But despite these successes—despite the fact that Al Qaida has been dramatically weakened—it has not been destroyed.

Some of the patterns of terrorism that we observe worldwide are a reflection of our success. In other words, certainly we are improving, certainly we are getting better, certainly international cooperation is at a higher level than it has been in the past. But at the same time, our adversaries have not concluded that it has become too difficult to ply their trade of violence and mayhem; they haven't concluded that it's too difficult to engage in terrorism and laid down their arms; they have not left the field. Rather, what we are witnessing is a constant process of adaptation and adjustment. And we see that our adversaries remain, not just determined, but formidable.

I think a very good case in point is the circular that was issued by the US Transportation Security Agency at the end of July 2003 stating that Al Qaida and associated groups were still developing means, were still attempting to seize commercial aircraft, hijack them and use them, in essence, as human cruise missiles.

Now this in itself is astonishing, because probably the one field, at least in the United States, where one can observe the greatest progress in physical security measures against terrorism is in commercial aviation. We have hardened the cockpit doors. We have made it far more difficult for terrorists to smuggle arms onto planes. And yet, in the very area where we have focused tremendous energy and resources in order to ensure that a tragedy like 9/11 cannot recur, terrorists continue to plot and plan to overcome and obviate precisely those defenses.

I think this fact is very important. Because what we must realize is that terrorism is highly dynamic—perhaps one of the most dynamic phenomena there is. In fact, in the past, I have compared the most determined and formidable of our terrorist adversaries to the archetypal shark in the water. In other words, the shark has to constantly move forward to survive. Terrorists must constantly plan and plot attacks to succeed, to elbow their way back into the limelight, to garner the publicity that they hope to parlay into intimidation and coercion. And what this means is that if terrorism is a dynamic phenomenon, so must our thinking about terrorism be dynamic, and even more importantly, so must our responses. Our responses have to be constantly reviewed, updated and adjusted. I'll come back to this at the end of my presentation. So that's the first broad point.

The second broad theme is that we are engaged in a war against terrorism, given the events of September 11th and the consequences of Al Qaida's ambitious nuclear, biological and chemical aims that were uncovered in Afghanistan. We know we are embroiled in a war against terrorism. But from an American perspective, I would say this is unlike any other conventional war that we ever fought. I think, all to the good, that in the United States we have become accustomed to wars that last months, if not weeks. The first Gulf War, as well as the initial military operations in Iraq, have been short and that is good.

But the problem is that our adversaries are not measuring this struggle in terms of weeks and months, or even years. They are thinking in decades. They view this as a fundamentally epic battle—a war of attrition. And what they are seeking to do is to wear down our resolve to resist them. They have confidence—and this is what sustains them, despite innumerable tactical defeats that we have inflicted upon them in the past two years. So that is the second point. We are entangled in a war of attrition.

Then, thirdly—having studied terrorism now for a quarter of a century, I can say that it was never an easy subject to understand—now it is becoming even harder to categorize and pigeonhole, and consequently more difficult to understand. This is why a conference on post-modern terrorism is so apt.

In the past nearly two years, Al Qaida has been weakened. But just as obviously, Al Qaida has not been destroyed. It is far too soon to write Al Qaida's obituary. What we face is not only a very determined and formidable adversary, but one that has shown itself to be extremely nimble, flexible and adaptive. What Al Qaida has done is to diversify. I think this was always the case: From the beginning, Al Qaida itself was conceived by Bin-Laden to function on at least four different operational levels. And this is precisely why Al Qaida is so hard to completely defeat today. I would argue that there exist not one Al Qaida, but many Al Qaidas.

This is one of the fundamental misconceptions about Al Qaida—one of the basic traps that we risk falling into when misreading this threat—that sometimes we refer to Al Qaida almost as we once did to the Soviet Union, as a monolithic force. But this is not the case. As I said, even as a specific entity, it functions on at least four operational levels.

You have the professional terrorist, the highly dedicated and trained terrorist such as Muhammad Atta, the 19 hijackers, those Al Qaida operatives who engage in the spectacular, high-value attacks such as the bombings of the U.S. Embassies in 1998, the attack on the U.S.S. Cole, and so on.

But there are also other levels. Right below the professionals, there is a level of what one might call the trained amateurs; people who trained in Al Qaida camps—people with a modicum of experience and skills but perhaps not quite the same dedication, and maybe not even the intelligence of Muhammad Atta and his confederates. And here I refer to Richard Reed, the inept shoe bomber, who attempted to blow up an American Airlines flight while en route from Paris to Miami in December, 2001. These people are trained—individuals who are part of Al Qaida—but are not necessarily functioning on a direct operational chain from the organization. There is may not be any direct command and control relationship from a core Al Qaida command and control cell. That is the second level.

You drop down to the third level, and there you have the panoply of associated or affiliated groups—those groups that Al Qaida trained. I think Rohan Gunaratna has described Afghanistan as "the Disneyland of terrorism." Over the past decade, nearly thousands of terrorists received training in Afghanistan, in the Sudan and in Yemen. They are involved in groups that are not Al Qaida specifically, and have their own local and regional agendas, but at the same time, are more than content to pursue Al Qaida's transnational goals.

And then you have a fourth level—the unaffiliated level—what I call the local walk-ins. These are Islamic radicals throughout the world who have no actual prior connection with Al Qaida, but are motivated and stimulated by Bin-Laden, by the calls to Jihad, by various events unfolding in the world today. Completely on their own, independently, they carry out acts that they feel will be of direct benefit to Al Qaida or to the war against the West.

I think this is why Al Qaida has proven so resilient and so difficult to vanquish. It is not one entity. Certainly, Al Qaida has been weakened, and I think the most important metric of success is the obvious one; the prevention of Al Qaida's attempts to carry out a spectacular attack, not just in the United States, but anywhere else in the world since 9/11. And we have seen that this achievement has lasted now for nearly two years. But at the same time—and here we come to one of the asymmetries of terrorism—beyond any doubt, Al

Qaida's ability and its associated and affiliated groups' ability to inflict pain at some level remains intact.

Now obviously, there's a world of difference between blowing up a bar in Bali on a Saturday night and laying the Twin World Trade Center Towers to waste or attacking the Pentagon. But at the end of the day, the outcome is the same: the tragic loss of innocent life. The terrorists fundamentally believe in the rejuvenating power of even a single successful terrorist operation to launch them back into the headlines, and enable them to crack their whip of intimidation and coercion: in other words, to cause us to behave differently, to have an effect.

It is immaterial to the terrorists whether or not there was a proven or actual cause and effect sequence for instance between the attacks that we witnessed in Saudi Arabia and Morocco in the beginning of May 2003, and the subsequent elevation of the threat level, the color-coding, from yellow to orange in the United States. What they see is cause and effect. They acted, we responded. And that is what convinces them that if they just continue to struggle, if they continue to attack, ultimately they will be victorious. I think we are learning, too, in the two years since September 11th and in the less than two years since the first phase of the war against terrorism in Afghanistan, in actual fact this country was not essential to Al Qaida's international terrorist capabilities. Admittedly, their ability to carry out September 11th-type spectaculars has been diminished, but what we have witnessed in the succession of terrorist attacks over the past year and a half demonstrates this remarkable resiliency once again. In the annals of the history of terrorism, probably no terrorist entity has had quite the amount of force applied against it like the scope of military power that Al Qaida experienced in Afghanistan at the hands of the United States and coalition forces. And yet, despite the punishment meted out to Al Qaida, the destruction of its training camps and operational bases, the ruin of its state within a state, the loss of its control over Afghanistan, within two months of the last set piece battle fought in January 2002 at Shah-e-Kot in the White Mountains, there was Al Qaida in March 2002, carrying out an international terrorist operation in Tunisia, the first of many. In that respect, I would argue that the three capabilities critical to 9/11, from Al Qaida's perspective, still exist. Its ability to identify and explore gaps in our defenses and security remains. As the TSA circular I referred to demonstrates, that process of endeavoring to identify and exploit gaps in our defenses is ongoing. Secondly, the use of deception and denial is still rampant. This is one reason why we so poorly understand Al Qaida. I would argue that this is due to its conscious policy of deception and denial. We have already observed that deception is one of Al Qaida's hallmarks. If anything, the operations on 9/11 were perhaps one of the greatest deception exercises in history. The passengers on board a plane thought it was a stereotypical traditional hijacking, where of course the standard operating procedure is to cooperate with the hijackers because that is the surest way to survive. But in fact, it was a ruse to turn those planes into human missiles.

And then, thirdly, there is the use of suicide attacks, which as we have observed since 9/11, has not diminished. So I think the patterns of terrorism and the trends that we are witnessing right now and are likely to see in the near future, are a succession of smaller, protracted acts worldwide as part of this global war of attrition in which we are now enmeshed, alongside Al Qaida's continuing desire to stage a spectacular operation.

Having discussed some of the key trends in terrorism, let us move on to the nature of our reaction to terrorism. And here I think that the world has a lot to learn from Israel. I think it is an important lesson, in fact, that the first incident of what we call modern terrorism is commonly agreed to have occurred (despite many disagreements among terrorism experts), on July 22 1968, when three Palestinian terrorists hijacked an El Al aircraft en route from Rome to Tel Aviv. And it is fascinating to look back on the newspaper accounts of that hijacking. For the rest of the world, this was something that was dismissed. This was regarded as something within the Palestinian-Israeli dynamic; it was declared a reflection of the always volatile, violent Middle East. And many people consoled themselves, believing that these problems regarding aviation security and terrorism would remain confined to Israel and to the Middle East, and would not spill over elsewhere. Certainly with 9/11 as the clear example, and as demonstrated by the circular dated two months ago, aviation security remains a formidable problem more than three decades later. This is why I think it is possible to study the intensification of terrorism that we have witnessed in Israel over the past three years, and glean relevant lessons for countries elsewhere. And here I observe four major watersheds that have occurred in Israel and are relevant to the international community. The first is the sustained nature of the suicide bombing campaign that has taken place in Israel. This point is very important. We know suicide bombing is nothing new; suicide attacks are not new. But what is new is the sustained, protracted nature of the phenomenon. In fact, according to thethe RAND chronology of terrorism , some 70% of suicide attacks against Israel have occurred within the past three years alone.. Suicide terrorism was once a sporadic, isolated, dramatic incident. In fact, Ariel Merari published an important paper in 1985, in which he stated that in Lebanon during the mid-1980's, only 17% of the Hizballah attacks were suicide attacks. The majority took other forms of terrorist operations. Not surprisingly, today terrorist groups increasingly favor suicide terrorism as a tactic because it is more lethal. According to RAND's figures, on an average, suicide terrorist attacks cause four times more casualties than other types of terror. According to our figures, too, in Israel suicide attacks claim about six times as many victims as other forms of terrorist attacks, and astonishingly injure 26 times more bystanders.

Secondly, another important watershed, which fortunately did not materialize, was the May 2002 attempt to blow up the gas facility at Pi-Glilot in Ramat Hasharon. Here we rightly concern ourselves with terrorists' use of chemical, biological, radiological or nuclear weapons, which would cause mass casualty events. The significance of that incident is that it was an attack against a dual-use target. It was aimed at an industrial target, not using an unconventional weapon but rather a very conventional weapon, and designed to lead to unconventional results, in other words, mass casualties. How many of our countries have similar types of industrial facilities close to major cities and suburbs that could be affected? Certainly, last November's surface-to-air missile attack on an Israeli aircraft in Mombassa is a universal warning. Some 53 countries throughout the world manufacture Stinger class missiles. This remains a big threat.

And finally, we have witnessed the increasing use of poisons by suicide terrorists in Israel, too, as well as the interest of groups like Hamas in the use of chemical weapons.

As I said at the beginning, I believe that the nature and character of terrorism is changing. It is becoming increasingly difficult to pigeonhole. In the past, terrorism was perpetrated by coordinated, tight organizations with a very defined and clear command and control structure. What we are currently observing is a phenomenon that is much more amorphous, more diffuse, and much more difficult to track. It has no clear footprint and almost no clear modus operandi. In particular, we must note the emergence not just of lone terrorists or lone perpetrators, but also of independent, small cells of perpetrators. For example, in the United States over the past decade (with the exception of the 1993 World Trade Center attack and 9/11), all of the most significant terrorist incidents were not committed by identifiable terrorist groups or organizations, but by lone individuals or by collections, or cells, of individuals acting independently: Theodore Kaczynski, the Unabomber; Timothy McVeigh, the Oklahoma City bombing; Eric Rudolph, the bomber of the 1996 Atlanta Olympics; the two Palestinians in 1997 who plotted a suicide attack on the New York City subway; and Hasham Hadayat who staged an attack on the El Al counter at LAX, the Los Angeles airport in July, 2002.

As we look to the future and as noted earlier, Al Qaida remains a poorly understood phenomenon, and this in itself is remarkable. Nearly two years after 9/11, more than a decade after this group emerged, it remains an enigma. But clearly, there are many Al Qaidas, not one.

In conclusion, the fundamental lesson to be drawn from 9/11, especially given that we are now embroiled in a war of attrition, is not to be lulled into a false sense of complacency or rest on past laurels. The challenge for us will be to retain our focus, maintain vigilance and keep up the pressure, even as we adjust to the changes and adaptations unfolding amongst terrorist groups worldwide.

This leads us to the fundamental asymmetry: The basic metric of success for terrorists is the ability to act and attack, to get back into the headlines and claim the limelight. The fundamental metric of success for governments is to prevent those attacks. For that reason, governments are only as good as their last success. This is why countering terrorism is a perennial, ceaseless struggle.

The New al-Qaida: Developments in the Post-9/11 Evolution of al-Qaida

Prof. Rohan K. Gunaratna

Institute for Defense & Strategic Studies, Singapore.

Why did al-Qaida attack America's iconic targets? Even three years after the watershed event, the rationale for al-Qaida's multiple attacks on America's most outstanding landmarks on 9/11 remains a riddle. The rationale for the attacks is enshrined in the founding charter of al-Qaida published *in Al Jihad*, the principal journal of the Arab mujahidin published in Peshawar, Pakistan in April 1988.

From the very beginning, al-Qaida Al Sulbah (The Solid Base), was, according to its Palestinian-Jordanian founder, Dr Abdullah Azzam, meant to be the "Pioneering Vanguard of the Islamist Movements." Despite deviations in strategy and tactics, Osama bin Laden, the deputy and protegé of Azzam, carried out the mandate of Azzam. Bin Laden directed the attack on America's most outstanding landmarks to inspire and incite the wider Muslim community and to show the way to the other Islamist movements. In the same way that the mujahidin "defeated" the Soviet army, the largest land army in the world, thus reducing the superpower of the Russian Empire to "tiny" Russia, al-Qaida intended to achieve a similar effect by conducting a wave of strikes against America and its interests overseas.

In reality, it was not the Arab mujahidin that checkmated the Soviet military but the Afghan mujahidin. Nonetheless, the Arab mujahidin that waged several decisive battles and brought in significant resources took credit, successfully instilling the belief in the Islamist movements and to a lesser extent in the Muslim world that the world's remaining superpower could also be targeted and destroyed.

With the US intervention in Afghanistan in October 2001, the international security environment changed dramatically. During the past two years, al-Qaida has suffered the destruction of its state-of-the-art training and operational infrastructure in Afghanistan; lost 60%-70% of its core and operational leadership; and 3,200 operatives in 102 countries have been captured.[1] Although al-Qaida's intention to attack has not diminished, its capability has suffered. Nonetheless, a robust Islamist milieu ensures that al-Qaida will be able to replenish its human losses and material wastage. To survive the US-led global hunt, al-Qaida has dispersed worldwide and sought sanctuary within associated Islamist groups fighting territorial and local campaigns worldwide. To compensate for the loss of Afghanistan, al-Qaida's principal training ground, its members are increasingly relying on the three-dozen Islamist groups it had financed, armed, trained and indoctrinated throughout the 1990s.

In its new role, al-Qaida is unifying, inspiring, instigating and coordinating attacks with disparate Islamist groups located in Asia, the Middle East, Africa and the Caucuses. With the dispersal of al-Qaida trainers, organizers of attacks, financiers and other operatives from the core of Pakistan and Afghanistan to lawless zones in the global south, these like-minded groups pose a threat comparable to al-Qaida. The New al-Qaida differs from the Old al-Qaida in size, structure, demography and strateegy.

Al-Qaida's role changed immediately prior to the Soviet withdrawal in February 1989. In addition to inheriting the anti-Soviet Afghan training and operational infrastructure, al-Qaida benefited from the worldwide network created by its predecessor Maktab-il-Khadimat (MAK: Afghan Service Bureau), with 30 offices in North America and Western Europe. As the international community neglected Afghanistan, the country that won the war against communism, and Pakistan, a frontline state in the battle against communism, both countries became international centers for ideological and

---

1   Considering its numerical strength of 4,000 members (estimated in October 2001), the loss of 3,200 members and key supporters is significant. The figure of 4,000 members is derived from Al Qaida detainee debriefs, including the FBI interrogation of Muhammad Mansour Jabarah, the twenty-one-year old Canadian operative of Kuwaiti-Iraqi origin detained in mainland USA since 2002.

physical combat training of Islamist guerrilla and terrorist groups. By the early 1990s, Afghanistan had replaced the Syrian controlled Bekka Valley as the principal center of international terrorism. As the West looked the other way, Afghanistan evolved into a "Terrorist Disneyland." Several Islamist groups, principally al-Qaida in cooperation with the Islamist Movement of the Taliban, the ruling party of the Islamic Emirate of Afghanistan, trained 70,000-130,000 mujahidin until the intervention of the US-led coalition in October 2001.

Al-Qaida provided trained recruits and funds to local Islamist groups fighting in conflict zones where Muslims were suffering including Tajikistan, Kashmir, Bosnia, Chechnya, Dagestan, Mindanao and Xingjiang. As the bulk of the Arab mujahidin, including its leader Bin Laden, was unwelcome in their home countries, they remained in Afghanistan and Pakistan. In the aftermath of the first World Trade Center attack in February 1993, when the US instructed Pakistan to expel the mujahidin or be declared a terrorist state, the bulk of the Arab mujahidin located in Pakistan migrated to Sudan when al-Qaida established its new headquarters there in December 1991. American and British pressure on Sudan forced al-Qaida to relocate to Afghanistan in May 1996, where Western intelligence agencies failed to monitor al-Qaida. After having established new relationships and consolidating old links with Balkan, Caucasian, Middle Eastern and East African groups when in Sudan, al-Qaida was able to develop closer and deeper ties with Asian groups after its relocation to Afghanistan. As an organization with a global membership, al-Qaida had diverse capabilities as well as access to unprecedented resources. Al-Qaida armed, trained, financed and indoctrinated three-dozen Islamist groups from Asia, Africa, the Middle East, and the Caucuses. In addition to its own training camps in Afghanistan, al-Qaida dispatched its own trainers to establish or serve in the training camps of other groups in Asia, Africa, the Middle East and the Caucuses.

Al-Qaida's distinct ideology of a universal jihad provided the framework for cooperation with disparate groups waging local and regional conflicts. In contrast to its associated groups, al-Qaida's all-inclusive ideology advocated a struggle that was not bound by territorial boundaries. Although these local and regional groups waged parochial struggles, their interaction with al-Qaida inspired commitment to fighting both their territorial and international enemies. As a part of the ideological training, in many cases al-Qaida successfully instilled that both the near and distant enemy must be targeted. In most cases, the near enemy was the "false Muslim rulers" and the "corrupt Muslim regimes," while the distant enemy was the United States. By defining the United States as the "head of the poisonous snake" protecting and shielding the false rulers and corrupt regimes in the Middle East, Bin Laden justified the attacks against the United States and its interests.

Two years after 9/11, is al-Qaida still the "spearhead of Islam"? Has al-Qaida lost its vanguard role in the aftermath of 9/11? Since the US led coalition's intervention in Afghanistan in October 2001, al-Qaida has lost its capacity to plan, prepare and execute operations on the scale of 9/11. Despite the fact that al-Qaida's human and material capability to attack has suffered, its intention to attack has not diminished. Al-Qaida has compensated for its traditional role by (a) working even more closely with like-minded Islamist groups and (b) aggressively propagating the al-Qaida ideology of the universal jihad.

The most profound development in al-Qaida's post 9/11 evolution is its steadfast reliance on local and regional Islamist movements worldwide to advance its aims. These Islamist political parties, guerrilla and terrorist groups located in Asia, Africa, the Middle East and the Caucuses maintain control over operational and support cells in North America, Europe and Australia. The Counter-Terrorism Center of the Central Intelligence Agency (CIA) accurately characterized al-Qaida as a "network of networks" prior to 9/11, but operationally al-Qaida developed the "network of networks" structure only after 9/11. The "network of networks" structure had been put in place prior to that date, but it was activated only subsequently. Rather than al-Qaida per se, post 9/11 al-Qaida—the New al-Qaida—is a network of groups influenced by al-Qaida. Al-Qaida's most enduring contribution to the sustenance of a long-range terrorist capability is the creation of a cadre of fighters that serves Islamist movements worldwide. During the last decade and a half, al-Qaida has created a threat of global proportions that will certainly outlast its lifespan.

Al-Qaida is partially compensating for its losses by working even more closely with its associate groups, relying on them for sanctuary, training new recruits and conducting operations. But most of all, al-Qaida is becoming an ideology—a state of mind. By resigning itself to a robust ideological and less operational structure, al-Qaida has increased its survivability. To compensate for its depleted operational capability, al-Qaida is investing extensively in sustained propaganda, inspiring and instigating the wider Muslim community, as well as other Islamist movements, to join in the fight against the United States and its allies. In effect, al-Qaida's new role includes promoting its traditional mission by non-military means through the mass media, especially the new communication technologies. The surge of regular pronouncements by Osama bin Laden and Ayman Al Zawahiri communicated by audio, video and print media since the US led coalition's intervention in Afghanistan in October 2001 has found resonance in the Muslim world especially following US intervention in Iraq in April 2003. Al-Qaida believes that it can only sustain the battle against the US and its allies by building a large committed support base throughout the Muslim world including in the diaspora and migrant communities. By continuing to politicize and radicalize the Muslims through the dissemination of propaganda, al-Qaida intends to increase the pool of recruits and support critical for the continuity of multiple group jihad programs.

Prior to 9/11, al-Qaida invested in propaganda but to a lesser degree. In the decade preceding 9/11, al-Qaida's primary mission was to train as many Muslims as possible and to provide specialized assistance to Islamist groups worldwide. Pre-9/11 virulent propaganda was primarily the responsibility of a number of Islamist parties and groups based in Europe and North America. After a number of these parties and groups came under the close scrutiny of Western governments, al-Qaida and its associated parties and groupstook over the role of information dissemination. In comparison to the pre-9/11 propaganda dominated by non al-Qaida groups, the al-Qaida brand of propaganda is extremely violent, directly calling on Muslims to kill. Al-Qaida's emphasis on ideological indoctrination and the lack of a counter ideology on the part of governments and society are inflicting severe long-term damage on the Muslim world. The political environment in Muslim countries is shifting in favor of Islamism and violence.

The Context

Since the emergence of the contemporary wave of terrorism in the Middle East in 1968, the world has witnessed three categories of terrorist organizations— ideological (left and right wing), ethno-nationalist (irredentist, separatist, autonomy) and politico-religious groups. Two landmark events—the Islamic revolution in Iran and the Soviet intervention in Afghanistan—(both in 1979) marked the emergence of the contemporary wave of Islamist guerrilla and terrorist groups.[2] While Iran's clerical regime held American diplomats hostage for 444 days in Tehran, the anti-Soviet multinational Afghan campaign checkmated the world's largest army—the Soviet army—in a protracted guerrilla campaign that latest a decade. While an Islamist regime defied one superpower in the Middle East, an Islamist movement defeated another superpower in Afghanistan. In response to the Soviet occupation of Afghanistan (December 1979-February 1989), US presence in the Arabian Peninsula (December 1990), Gulf War I (January 1991) and the US-led coalition occupation of Iraq (March 2003), Islamism grew in strength, size and influence. As a result, virulent and extremist ideologies found greater acceptance, existing Islamist political parties and terrorist groups became more influential, and new Islamist organizations proliferated.

From the time of its foundation in March 1988, one year prior to the withdrawal of the Soviet troops from Afghanistan, al-Qaida built a "network of networks."[3] By co-opting leaders of like-minded Islamist movements, al-Qaida built an umbrella over which Osama bin Laden gradually assumed leadership. In its earlier life—Maktab-il-Khidamat (the Afghan Service

---

2   While guerrilla groups target combatants, terrorist groups target non-combatants.

3   The term was coined by the Counter-Terrorism Center at the Central Intelligence Agency, Langley, Virginia, USA some time in the late 1990s. Michael Sheehan, former US Ambassador for Counter – Terrorism and currently Deputy Commissioner for Counter-Terrorism at the New York Police Department, Seniors' Conference, US Military Academy, West Point, June 2003.

Bureau established in 1984)—built a global network that channeled resources and recruits from around the world to Afghanistan. After defeating the Soviet Army, the largest land army in the world, and stripping the Soviet Empire of its superpower status, the Islamists aimed their sights at the remaining superpower—the United States of America. As the vicious by-product of the anti-Soviet multinational Afghan campaign, al-Qaida had inherited a state-of-the-art training infrastructure, wealthy sponsors, proven trainers, experienced combatants and a vast support base stretching from Australia throughout the Muslim world into Canada.

After its victory against the Soviet army in Afghanistan in the 1980s, al-Qaida was transformed from a guerrilla group to a terrorist group capable of operating in urban terrain and targeting civilians after its headquarters relocated from Peshawar, Pakistan, to Khartoum, Sudan in December 1991. After the 1993 meeting in Khartoum between Osama bin Laden and Imad Mugneyev, Head of the Special Security Apparatus of Hizballah, the most dangerous terrorist group at that time, al-Qaida members and recruits received terrorist instruction in Sudan and Southern Lebanon.[4] The camps in Sudan were sponsored and conducted by the Iranian Ministry of Intelligence and Security Affairs (MOIS) and the Iranian Revolutionary Guards Corps (IRGC). As the Taliban regime perceived the clerical regime in Iran as inimical, Iranian sponsorship declined after Osama bin Laden relocated from Sudan to Afghanistan in May 1996.[5] After the US occupation of Iraq in March 2003, Iran became the immediate neighbor of the United States of America. When conducting its operations from Afghanistan, a landlocked country, al-Qaida had to rely either on Pakistan or Iran as a launching pad. With severe losses on its Pakistani front, since October 2001 al-Qaida has opened a new staging

---

4　The meeting was arranged by the former Egyptian Army Captain Ali Muhammad, who subsequently became a naturalized American citizen, joined the US military and served as a Supplies Sergeant at Fort Bragg, North Carolina, before joining Al Qaida and becoming the chief bodyguard of Osama bin Laden and Al Qaida's principal instructor, both in Afghanistan and Sudan. He is currently in US custody in mainland USA.

5　However, 10% of all phone calls from Osama bin Laden's satellite phone were to Iran between 1996-1998.

area, the Iranian front. Is Iran turning a blind eye to al-Qaida or actively supporting it? If the latter is true, exactly which Iranian agency in its fractured government is supportive of al-Qaida? There are early signs of covert Iranian sponsorship of al-Qaida, but this may be coming from only one segment of the fractured government. As its immediate neighbor, both Iran and Syria, sponsors of the Lebanese Hizballah, perceive the United States of America as a severe threat as well as its number one enemy, a notion shared by both al-Qaida and Hizballah, the leading Shiite and Sunni terrorist groups today.

Al-Qaida has suffered formidable losses since September 11, 2001. Nonetheless, the robust Islamist milieu in which al-Qaida operates has enabled the group to replenish its human losses, i.e. members captured and killed, as well as material wastage, i.e., assets seized and funds frozen. Furthermore, having imparted guerilla and terrorist training to several tens of thousands of Islamists from around the world in its camps in Afghanistan, al-Qaida built up sufficient strategic depth worldwide to generate support and recruits. As a well-endowed and well-resourced group from its inception, al-Qaida invested in creating a cadre of highly dedicated and committed fighters willing to kill and die in the name of religion. Whether they live in the West or East, al-Qaida supporters and sympathizers believe in the often repeated al-Qaida dictum: "It is the duty of every Muslim to wage jihad."

Despite the US-led intensive and sustained global hunt, al-Qaida continues to constitute an unprecedented threat. Its unique historical origins, religious character, and organizational structure guarantee its sustenance and survival. When compared with all the other terrorist groups that we have been studying since the emergence of the contemporary wave of terrorism in 1968, al-Qaida is different in composition, diversity and reach. With the exception of Aum Shinrikyo of Japan, al-Qaida is the first multinational terrorist group of the 21st century.[6] It has recruited activists from the Muslim territories of Asia, Africa, the Middle East, Caucuses and the Balkans as well as the Muslim migrant and diaspora communities of Europe, North America and Australia. In contrast to

---

6   It should be noted that Aum Shinrikyo does not have the same global composition or the global reach of Al Qaida.

other groups that have recruited from one single nationality[7] or groupings of nationalities from one particular region,[8] al-Qaida is truly multinational. Despite global efforts to detect, disrupt, degrade and destroy al-Qaida, the group has survived because it has a global presence. Periodically it has attacked symbolic, strategic and high profile targets across geographic regions to make its presence known to its support base and to its enemies. Its capacity to survive is largely due to its loosely networked structure, diverse composition and universal ideology. To counter and evade the growing threat to al-Qaida, the group itself has transmuted structurally, strategically and geographically. Al-Qaida is global in reach, from Asia to Canada; and multi-national in composition, from Uigurs in Xinjiang to American Hispanics: It therefore enjoys diverse capabilities, access to resources, and multiple modus operandi. There is no standard textbook for fighting al-Qaida. To effectively destroy a group like al-Qaida, a global approach and a global strategy are prerequisites.

Post-9/11 al-Qaida

Today, al-Qaida is in a period of transition. It temporary lost its base—Afghanistan—and its host, the Islamist Movement of the Taliban, the ruling party of the Islamic Emirate of Afghanistan. More significantly, the death or capture of the bulk of its operational leaders, members and key supporters has dented its operational effectiveness. Despite the dismantling of its training and operational infrastructure in Afghanistan, al-Qaida is adapting by seeking to establish bases elsewhere. It therefore remains a serious, immediate and direct threat to its enemies. Although al-Qaida's physical and personnel infrastructure worldwide has suffered, its multi-layered global network still

---

7   For instance, Egyptian Islamic Jihad and the Islamic Group of Egypt has only Egyptian members; The Armed Islamic Group of Algeria and Salafi Group for Call and Combat have only Algerians members, the Moro Islamic Liberation Front and the Abu Sayaaf Group have only Moros as members.

8   For instance, Takfir Wal Hijra, a group active in Europe and North America recruited from North Africa—Egyptians, Algerians, Libyans, Algerians, Moroccans, and Tunisians—and Jemmah Islamiyah recruited from Southeast Asia and Australia—Indonesian, Malaysian, Thais, Singaporeans, Filipinos, and Australians (both cradle and converted Muslims).

retains sufficient depth to plan, prepare and execute operations directly and through associate groups. By ideologically and physically penetrating a number of regional conflicts in which Muslims participate, al-Qaida's decentralized network works with like-minded groups. Following sustained action by the US and its allies in Afghanistan and Pakistan, the core of al-Qaida, its attack organizers, trainers, financiers, operatives and other experts are moving to lawless zones in Asia, the Middle East, the Horn of Africa and the Caucuses.

Like the aftereffect of a strike on a beehive, al-Qaida members are gravitating and seeking new bases in Mindanao in the Philippines, the Bangladesh-Myanmar border, Yemen, Somalia, Pankishi Valley in Georgia and Chechnya. Much like the shark that rapidly moves in search of new prey, post-9/11 al-Qaida cells survive and strike given the opportunity. After identifying the weaknesses and the loopholes of the new security architecture, a constantly probing al-Qaida is likely to infiltrate. While retaining a presence in Afghanistan, post 9/11 al-Qaida members are active and its fresh recruits train in conflict zones. For al-Qaida, regional conflicts are healthy green houses to rebuild, regroup and strike.

Although al-Qaida as an organization per se has suffered, it is still retaining its pioneering vanguard status among the Islamist movements. In keeping with the founding charter authored by its founder and leader Dr Abdullah Azzam, al-Qaida remains the spearhead of the Islamist movements. Despite repeated high-quality losses, al-Qaida is still able to set the ideological and operational agenda for three-dozen foreign Islamist groups that it trained and financed during the last decade. Al-Qaida is able to preserve its global status by relying on its associated groups to sustain its struggle against the US and its allies. To compensate for the loss of its state-of-the-art training infrastructure in Afghanistan, al-Qaida is exploiting the Islamist movements within its ideological, military and financial spheres of influence. Up until the US intervention in October 2001, international neglect of Afghanistan turned the country into a "terrorist Disneyland," with about 40 Islamist groups receiving both guerrilla and terrorist training throughout the 1990s. These

Asian, Middle Eastern, African and Caucasian groups, which hitherto fought local campaigns, were influenced by al-Qaida's vision of a global jihad and today pose a threat comparable to that of al-Qaida.

The post 9/11 trajectory of al-Qaida operations demonstrates its staying power. Following sustained US and allied action in Afghanistan and Pakistan, al-Qaida has demonstrated an infinite capacity to change its shape. In the coming months, al-Qaida will fragment, decentralize, regroup in lawless zones of the world, work with like-minded groups, select a wider range of targets, focus on economic targets and population centers, and conduct most attacks in the global south. Although the group will be constrained from conducting coordinated simultaneous attacks against high profile, symbolic or strategic targets in the West, together with its regional counterparts al-Qaida will attack in Asia, Africa, the Middle East and even in Latin America, a region where it has only a limited presence. Despite the likely capture or death of its core and penultimate leaders, al-Qaida's anti-Western universal jihad ideology inculcated among the politicized and radicalized Muslims will sustain support for al-Qaida.

While its attack organizers will remain in Pakistan and Iran, its operatives and messengers will travel back and forth, coordinating with al-Qaida nodes in safe zones such as Yemen, Somalia, Bangladesh, the Philippines and Chechnya. To make its presence felt, al-Qaida will increasingly rely on its global terrorist network of groups in Southeast Asia, South Asia, the Horn of Africa, the Middle East, and the Caucuses to strike out at its enemies. Already attacks in Kenya, Indonesia, India, Pakistan, Kuwait and Yemen seek to compensate for the loss and lack of space and opportunity to operate in the West. Its operatives are currently working together with Jemmah Islamiyah (JI: Southeast Asia), Al Ithihad al Islami (Horn of Africa), Al Ansar Mujahidin (Caucuses), the Tunisian Combatants Group (Middle East), Jayash-e-Muhammad (South Asia), the Salafi Group for Call and Combat (GSPC, North Africa, Europe and North America), and other Islamist groups it trained and financed in the past decade. As al-Qaida has a very small number of cells in the West, the group will operate through the GSPC and Takfir Wal Hijra—two groups it infiltrated into Europe and North America.[9] With the transfer of terrorist technology and expertise from the center to the periphery, the attacks by the associated groups of al-Qaida pose a threat comparable to that of al-Qaida.

The fragmentation of al-Qaida support and operational infrastructure, under sustained military and law enforcement action, is inducing it to rely on the diversity of its strategic linkages and global reach. The decentralization of al-Qaida has contributed to its flexibility of targeting. Despite being the most hunted terrorist group in history, its cellular structure, rigid compartmentalization and the robust Islamist milieu ensure its resilience against destruction. Following the sustained military action in Afghanistan, the threat of terrorism has diffused, thus increasing the threshold for political violence worldwide. The new threshold of terrorism is a multidimensional, complex and global challenge. Despite sustained attrition of Islamist networks since October 2001, their high capacity for replenishing losses by regenerating fresh support and recruits has ensured the continuity of the intellectual and operational capabilities of al-Qaida. This being the case, many governments and publics will have to live with a medium to high threat index for several years in different parts of the world.

In response to the high threat to al-Qaida, the group is becoming more creative and lethal. The group is adapting dual technologies—airplanes, commercially available chemicals, agricultural fertilizers, liquid petroleum gas, and liquid nitrogen gas—as its new weapons. The group is also searching for new weapons such as chemical and biological agents, especially contact poisons that are easy to conceal and breach security. Both Osama's statement in February 2003 "think intelligently and kill the Americans secretly" and Sheikh Nasr bin Hamid al Fahd's May 2003 fatwa legitimize the use of chemical, biological, radiological and nuclear weapons.[10] Although an attempt to pervert Islam, it

---

9   Hasan Hattab the head of the European network of the Armed Islamic Group of Algeria (GIA) broke away from the GIA in 1998 and formed the GSPC. Although the GSPC is stronger in Europe, a cell in the US planning to target the MGM hotel and casino in Las Vegas was apprehended by the FBI in 2002.

10   Interview, Dr Reuven Paz, International Policy Institute for Counter-Terrorism, Israel, May 2003.

is likely that the Saudi Sheik presented Koranic justifications, a requirement in Islam, as a prelude to an attack. Reflecting the existing and emerging threat, Eliza Manningham-Buller, Head of the British Security Services (MI5), said in London on July 17,2003 that a terrorist attack on a Western city using chemical, biological, radiological and nuclear (CBRN) technology is "only a matter of time."[11] She added: "We know that renegade scientists have cooperated with al Qaida and provided them with some of the knowledge they need to develop these weapons."[12] An al-Qaida associate group, the Salafi Group for Call and Combat (GSPC), successfully developed ricin, one of the contact poisons mentioned in the al-Qaida manuals, and its rudimentary manufacturing apparatus in London in January 2003. The ricin network in Europe, particularly in London, Manchester, East Anglia and Edinburgh in the UK, cooperated with al-Qaida experts in the Pankishi Gorge in Georgia, on the border of Chechnya.

In the current environment, terrorist groups will continue to recruit and instruct its members and supporters living in the West to support and conduct attacks. With the exception of the bombing of the Federal Building in Oklahoma in 1995, almost all of the major terrorist attacks in the West have been conducted by members of diaspora and migrant communities. The 9/11 coordinator, Ramzi bin al Shibh, and the suicide pilots were migrants living in the West. As foreign terrorist groups based in North America, Western Europe and Australia did not pose a direct or immediate threat to Western security until 9/11, these host governments tolerated their activity and presence. Even after 9/11, due to the reluctance of Europe, Canada and Australia to disrupt terrorist support networks, terrorist organizations continue to target 'migr' communities for recruits and support. In addition to al-Qaida front, cover and sympathetic groups, other Islamist groups are aggressively politicizing, radicalizing and mobilizing their migrants and diaspora. Assif Muhammad Hanif, 21, and Omar Khan Sharif, 27, two British suicide bombers of Asian

---

11 Eliza Manningham-Buller, Terrorism Conference, Royal United Services Institute, London, July 17, 2003.

12 Ibid

origin from Derbyshire UK, infiltrated Israel and attacked Mike's Place, a nightclub, on April 30 2003. While Hanif detonated, killing two musicians and one waiter and injuring 60, Sharif's explosive device failed to detonate. Since the beginning of the 31-month uprising in Israel, Hanif's bombing was the first suicide attack perpetrated by a foreigner. Similarly, in Asia, the first suicide bomber who targeted the State Assembly in Srinagar, Kashmir was a British Muslim, also of Asian origin. The 'migr' communities remain vulnerable to ideological penetration, recruitment, and provision of financial support. Despite stepped up government surveillance, disenfranchised segments of the emigre communities in Western countries still identify themselves with the struggles in their homelands. Until and unless host governments develop a better understanding of the threat and make an effort to target terrorist propaganda, both its tools and its ideologies, the threat to the West from within will persist.

As illustrated by statements issued by both Osama bin Laden and his successor and deputy Dr Ayman Al Zawahiri, although al-Qaida's capability to attack the West has diminished, its intention to attack has not. On October 6 2002, Osama bin Laden, the Emir-General of al-Qaida, said: "I am telling you, and God is my witness, whether America escalates or de-escalates this conflict, we will reply to it in kind, God willing. God is my witness, the youth of Islam is willing, and preparing things that will fill your hearts with tears. They will target the key sectors of your economy until you stop your injustice and aggression or until the more short-lived of the US die."[13] Ayman Al Zawahiri said on Al Jazeera Television on October 8, 2002: "Our message to our enemies is this: America and its allies should know that their crimes will not go unpunished, God willing. We advise them to hasten to leave Palestine, the Arabian Peninsula, Afghanistan, and all Muslim countries, before they lose everything. We addressed some messages to America's allies to stop their involvement in its crusader campaign. The Mujahid youths have addressed a message to Germany and another to France. If these measures have not been

---

13 Osama bin Laden's two-minute audiotape broadcast marking the first anniversary of the US intervention in Afghanistan, Al Jazeera, Arab Satellite Television Station, Qatar, October 6, 2002.

sufficient, we are ready with the help of God, to increase them."[14] In many ways, their periodic pronouncements and statements are the best guide to future al-Qaida actions.

Having recruited members from a cross-section of society—the rich, the poor, the educated and the less educated, al-Qaida has developed a reasonably good understanding of Western security measures and countermeasures. After the bombing of the US embassies in East Africa in August 1998, the US government enhanced the perimeter security of its land targets. Then in October 2000, al-Qaida attacked the USS Cole, a maritime target. When the US government enhanced the perimeter of its land and maritime targets, al-Qaida attacked America's icons from the sky. The tactical trajectory of al-Qaida suggests a cunning foe always keen to harass, injure and humiliate the enemy by deception.

Al-Qaida's tactical repertoire has been deeply influenced by the Iranian-sponsored Lebanese Hizballah. The Hizballah's modus operandi of coordinated simultaneous suicide attacks significantly influenced al-Qaida's modus operandi. As al-Qaida's aim was also to force the withdrawal of US troops from the Arabian Peninsula, the group emulated the Hizballah's success in Beirut in 1983, when the group forced the US-led multinational peace-keeping force to withdraw from Lebanon, following coordinated simultaneous suicide attacks on US and French targets. In the attack on its marine barracks, the US lost 243 personnel, the single largest loss since Vietnam. As a result, for several years the US disengaged itself from the politics of the Middle East. With the exception of the attack on the USS Cole, all the mega attacks by al-Qaida have taken the form of coordinated simultaneous suicide attacks. For instance, al-Qaida attacked the US Embassies in Kenya and Tanzania in August 1998; it attempted to destroy the Los Angeles international airport, the Radisson Hotel in Amman, Jewish and Christian holy sites in Jordan, and the USS The Sullivans in Aden, Yemen on the eve of the Millennium; it attacked America's most outstanding economic and military facilities, and attempted

---

14 Ayman Al Zawahiri's question and answer exchange with an unidentified reporter, Al Jazeera, October 8, 2002.

to attack its political landmarks on 9/11. Similarly, al-Qaida influenced its associated groups to conduct coordinated simultaneous attacks. For instance, Jemmah Islamiyah successfully attacked 16 churches in Indonesia on Christmas Day in 2000 and five targets in Manila, Philippines on December 30, 2000.

In the early 1990s, al-Qaida's aim was to create Islamist states in the Middle East by targeting the false Muslim rulers and the corrupt Muslim regimes. After suffering significant losses, both to its operatives and assets in the Middle East, al-Qaida decided to abandon its policy of targeting nearby targets in favor of targeting the distant enemy—the West—especially the "head of the poisonous snake," the USA. Gradually, al-Qaida attacks escalated in intensity and sophistication—East Africa in August 1998, the USS Cole in October 2000, and America's mainland on 9/11. The two waves of attacks in October 2001 and May 2003 are major turning points. Today, al-Qaida is returning to its closer targets in the Middle East, Asia, Africa and the Caucuses. Having sustained significant damage to its support and operational infrastructure in North America, Western Europe and Australia, the primary target countries in the last two years, al-Qaida is aggressively seeking Western and Jewish targets in the Muslim World.

Although attacking inside North America, Europe, Australia and Israel remains a priority, Western security measures and countermeasures have made it expensive and difficult for al-Qaida to mount an operation on Western soil. Nonetheless, al-Qaida and its associate groups will attack Western targets outside the West where security is largely in the hands of foreign governments. Al-Qaida finds it less costly to operate in parts of Asia, Africa and the Middle East, where there are less stringent security controls. Therefore, most attacks will be against Western targets located in the global south such as the attack in Saudi Arabia. While focusing on Western targets, al-Qaida will continue to conduct operations against Muslim rulers and regimes supporting the US led "war on terror." The physical security of the Saudi royalty and the Pakistani and Afghan leaders Musharaaf and Karzai respectively, will remain particularly vulnerable and their regimes will come under sustained political challenges in the coming years.

With the hardening of US targets, the threat is shifting to both government and population targets belonging to US allies. Similarly, al-Qaida is increasingly looking for opportunity targets. For instance, when al-Qaida failed to target a US warship off Yemen, it targeted a French oil super tanker in October 2002. The hardening of government land and commercial aerial targets has shifted al-Qaida's focus to both soft land and maritime targets. Although al-Qaida's primary intention is to attack inside the US, it lacks quality operatives of Muhammad Atta's caliber to operate there. Therefore, al-Qaida is targeting US land, sea and aviation overseas. Increased hardening of US military and diplomatic targets after 9/11 is steadfastly shifting the threat to other classes of targets. For instance, al-Qaida cells in Morocco attempted to target both British and US shipping in the Straits of Gibraltar in mid 2002. Due to perimeter and structural hardening of Israeli and US Embassies in Europe and Asia, al-Qaida decided to target Israeli and the US allies. Today, more than ever before, US allies are vulnerable to al-Qaida attacks.

Hardening of government targets will also transfer the threat to softer targets, making civilians prone to terrorist attack. For instance, al-Qaida planned to attack US diplomatic targets in Bangkok, Singapore, Kuala Lumpur, Phnom Penh, Hanoi and Manila, the American Institute in Taiwan, and the US consulate in Surabaya in September 2002,[15] but a visible security presence made the group consider softer targets. Although not in all cases, the hardening of targets works, but as the world has witnessed with horror, counter measures make terrorists creative and innovative. As the traditional explosives laden vehicle was a non-option to breach the hardened perimeter security of America's most outstanding landmarks, al-Qaida was forced to develop an aerial airborne capability. Similarly, hardening of military and diplomatic targets in Southeast Asia prompted Jemmah Islamiyiah to seek entertainment targets such as Bali. The reality is that government countermeasures have

---

15 Debriefing of Umar Al Faruq, detained at the Baghram Airbase in Afghanistan on September 9 2002, enabled the US government to issue an alert immediately before September 11 2002, the first anniversary of 9/11. Tactical Interrogation Report/ Umar Al Faruq, CIA, Langley, September 2002.

increased the vulnerability of population centers and economic targets. As Islamist groups weaken, they are likely to hit soft targets, killing civilians, if possible en masse. As it is impossible to prevent bombing of public places, civilian and civilian infrastructure targets will remain the most vulnerable to terrorist attack in the immediate, mid and long term.

Hardening of land and aviation targets will shift the threat to sea targets, particularly to commercial maritime targets. As any aviation incident attracts significant attention, al-Qaida attributes a high priority to aviation-impact terrorism. Due to the difficulty of hijacking aircraft to ram them against targets, al-Qaida will increasingly invest in conducting stand-off attacks and use hand held Surface-to-Air Missiles (SAMs). For instance, an al-Qaida Sudanese member fired a SA-7 missile at a US military transport plane at the Prince Sultan base in Saudi Arabia in mid-2001. His arrest in Khartoum in December 2001 led the Saudi authorities to locate another complete missile system buried in the Riyadh desert. If appropriate and immediate countermeasures are not taken to target the al-Qaida shipping network, SAMs under al-Qaida control being held in the Pakistan-Kashmir-Afghanistan theatre, the Arabian Peninsula, and the Horn of Africa will find their way to Far Asia and Europe, and possibly even to North America. Protective measures, such as target hardening of vulnerable government personnel and infrastructure by law enforcement and protective services are only a stopgap solution. To reduce the threat, governments have no option but to hunt terrorists and combat public support and sympathy for terrorism.

The post 9/11 robust security architecture has forced al-Qaida to alter its targeting strategy. Al-Qaida's capacity to conduct spectacular or theatrical attacks has diminished due to three factors: First, heightened human vigilance. The high state of alertness adopted by public and law enforcement authorities has led to the disruption of several operations. For instance, the alert passengers and crew prevented the bombing of the transatlantic flight by Richard Reid, the al-Qaida shoe bomber on board American Airlines no. 63 on December 22, 2001. Second, unprecedented law enforcement, security and intelligence cooperation and coordination. As a direct result of inter and intra agency cooperation, a large number of suspects have been detained and arrested, and over 100 attacks by al-Qaida and its associated groups have been interdicted, prevented or abandoned since 9/11. Cooperation beyond the Anglo-Saxon countries, Europe and Israel, especially with the Middle East and Asia, has led to significant arrests. For instance, Jose Padilla, who intended to mount surveillance and reconnaissance in order to detonate a radiological dispersal device in Washington D.C., was arrested en-route from Pakistan via Zurich at the Chicago O'Hare international airport in the US on May 8, 2002. Third, hunting al-Qaida and its associate groups has restricted their time, space and resources to conceptualize, plan and prepare elaborate terrorist strikes. As long as the international community can keep up the public vigilance, anti- and counter-terrorism cooperation and coordination worldwide and exert sustained pressure on the group, al-Qaida will not be able to mount large-scale coordinated simultaneous attacks on symbolic, strategic and high profile targets. Large attacks require long-term planning and preparation by several operatives across several countries. In the current security environment, where there are periodic desertions, arrests, and penetration, a terrorist group can only plan, prepare and execute small- to medium-scale operations. Preventing complacency from setting in, especially after a long period of al-Qaida inactivity, is difficult but it is mandatory if we are to prevent the next attack.

The nature of the al-Qaida threat has clearly changed since 9/11. In comparison, the post 9/11 threat to the US, its allies and its supporters is fragmented and diffused. Although it has no resources to carry out theatrical or spectacular attacks, it has a clandestine network to transfer experts, messages and money to associate groups. All indications show that al-Qaida is not deserting the 1520-mile long Pakistan-Afghanistan border, and its leadership is actively and aggressively tasking its membership and indoctrinating associate groups.[16]

---

16   Kashmir, only six hours by car from Afghanistan and the theatre of conflict nearest to Afghanistan, was visited by the author in August 2002. Both reviewing detainee tactical interrogation reports and debriefing of foreign detainees by the author revealed that Al Qaida is neither abandoning nor deserting Afghanistan or Pakistan, and the routine flow of foreigners to fight in Indian Kashmir continues uninterrupted.

From the center of Afghanistan and Pakistan, al-Qaida's technical experts and financiers, organizers of attacks and operatives are gravitating to lawless zones in Asia, the Horn of Africa, the Caucuses, the Balkans and the Middle East, thereby widening the perimeter of the conflict. Regional groups, such as Jemmah Islamiyah, and local groups, such as the Islamic Army of Abyan Aden, provide a platform for al-Qaida to plan, prepare and execute operations against Western targets and Muslim countries friendly to the West. For instance, the attack on the French oil tanker Limbourg was staged by al-Qaida, in cooperation with the Islamic Army of the Abyan in Aden. Similarly, the Bali bombing was staged by Jemmah Islamiya, working together with al-Qaida experts. Likewise, in Pakistan, a dozen attacks have been perpetrated by al-Qaida through individual members of Jaish-e-Mohommed, Lashkar-e-Jhangvi, Harakat-ul-Jihad-I-Islami, Lashkar-e-Tayyaba and Harakat-ul Mujahidin.[17] A decentralized al-Qaida working with Islamic and other groups worldwide is a force multiplier. In the years ahead, al-Qaida—which has a long history of providing experts, trainers and funds to other groups—is likely to operate effectively and efficiently through its associates. To compensate for the losses suffered by the group, post-9/11 al-Qaida operatives are heavily reliant on the social and familial contacts in associate groups. Therefore, mapping the family and social trees of leaders, members, supporters and sympathizers is the key to understanding the deepening operational nexus between al-Qaida and its associate groups. This nexus has manifested itself in tactical and opportune targeting, as well as in the globalization of the terrorist strategy,

---

17 For instance, the 9/11 mastermind Khalid Sheikh Muhammad, head of Al Qaida's military committee, assigned Jayashi-e-Mohommad member Ahmed Saeed Omar Sheikh the task of killing Daniel Pearl, the first US casualty in a terrorist attack since 9/11. Operating through Lashkar-e-Omar, an umbrella group mooted by Al Qaida, six terrorists opened fire and killed 17 Christians, including five children and a policeman, and injured 17 in a church in Bahawalpur, Punjabon October 28, 2001. Similarly, a grenade attack on a church in the heavily guarded diplomatic enclave in Islamabad killed 5, including a US official's wife and daughter, and injured 41 on March 17, 2002. Al Qaida also financed a car bombing to kill President Musharaff, and when it failed used the same car bomb to attack the US consulate. While Pakistanis mounted reconnaissance and organized the explosives and the vehicle, an Arab Al Qaida member arrived to perpetrate the suicide bombing, killing 12 Pakistanis and injuring 51, including one US marine guard in Karachi on June 14 2002.

developments that call for closer political, diplomatic, law enforcement, military, security and intelligence cooperation and coordination.

Wave Attacks

Today, al-Qaida conducts two types of attacks—stand-alone attacks and wave attacks. To achieve maximum impact and effect, al-Qaida prefers to perpetrate attacks in waves. The first wave of attacks by al-Qaida after 9/11 took place in October and November 2003, when al-Qaida, working together with the Islamic Army of the Abayan in Yemen, Jemmah Islamiyah in Indonesia (Islamic Group), Al Ansar Mujahidin in Chechnya (The Supporters of the Warriors of God); Shurafaa al-Urdun (The Honorables of Jordan) and Al Ittihad Al Islami (Islamic Union), staged five attacks. A suicide boat meant for a US warship attacked the French oil tanker Limbourg off Mukalla, Yemen on October 6; gunmen killed two US marines on exercises in Failaka, Kuwait on October 8; multiple suicide bombings took place in Bali, Indonesia on October 12, 2003; hostages were taken in a theatre in Moscow on October 24; USAID official Lawrence Foley was assassinated in Amman, Jordan on October 28; a suicide bombing was perpetrated at the Israeli owned Kikambala Paradise hotel, and a Surface-to-Air Missile attack was launched on Israeli Arkia Flight 582 on November 28.

After maintaining a year of silence, al-Qaida presented Koranic justifications in October 2002 immediately before launching the coordinated multiple attacks in the Middle East and Asia. The attacks in Yemen, Kuwait and Jordan demonstrated the ability of al-Qaida and its associated groups to function amidst security countermeasures. Islamist groups in Chechnya and Thailand also conducted terrorist operations in Russia and in Southern Thailand respectively. On October 6, an explosives laden suicide boat rammed the 157,833-ton French oil tanker Limbourg before mooring at al Shihr off the coast of Yemen. The explosion killed one Bulgarian and injured one-crew member, and caused the leakage of 90,000 barrels of crude oil.[18] Although

---

18 Al Qaida website al.neda.com claimed that it attacked the "French oil tanker off the coast of Yemen."

the exact time and location of the attack could not be determined, governments in Asia and in the Middle East had anticipated maritime suicide attacks on military and commercial shipping in the Straits of Malacca and in the Persian Gulf by al-Qaida.[19] Based on the debriefing of al-Qaida operatives detained in the Middle East and in Asia, the US intelligence community issued warnings regarding impending attacks. For instance, in anticipation of US and Indonesian joint military and naval exercises scheduled from May 30-June 3 2002, al-Qaida's former Southeast Asian representative Omar Al Faruq endeavored to locate terrorists to conduct suicide attacks against US warships in Surabaya, Indonesia's second largest city, in May 2002.[20] Two days after the Limbourg attack, two terrorists in a pickup truck attacked a marine unit of the US military on training maneuvers on Failaka, an island 10 miles east of Kuwait city.[21] The October 8 attack killed 20-year-old Lance Corporal Antonio J. Sledd from Hillsborough County, Florida. The terrorists drove to a second location to launch another attack but were killed by US marines.

Al-Qaida, operating through Jemmah Islamiyah (JI) in its Southeast Asian network, staged a grave terrorist attack in Indonesia's tourist resort of Bali, killing 202 and injuring over 300 people, mostly Australian tourists, on October 12, 2002—the anniversary of the USS Cole attack.[22] Before and after the mass-casualty bombing at the Sari Club, Bali at 23:15, small bombs exploded near other targets reflecting both al-Qaida and JI modus operandi and widespread capability to conduct coordinated simultaneous or near-simultaneous attacks. The targets were the Philippine Consulate, Manado City, North Sulawesi, at 18:45, the Paddy Restaurant at the Kuta Beach Strip in Bali at 23:00, and the vicinity of the US Consulate in Denpasar, Bali at

---

19 Terrorist connections of Abubakar Basyir; and further details on terrorist connections and
    activities of Umar Faruq, Orange Alert Document, September 2002, p. 2.

20 Umar Faruq's Terrorist Activities in Indonesia, Badan Inteligen Nasional (BIN: National
    Intelligence Agency), Jakarta, June 2002, p.1.

21 al.neda.com claimed that it attacked the "Fialka base in Kuwait"

22 al.neda.com claimed that it attacked the "nightclubs and whorehouses in Indonesia."

23.25.[23]   Bali, a predominately Hindu city where 22,000 Australians were holidaying, was the ideal target for JI-al-Qaida. The neighboring Philippines witnessed five bombings killing 22, including a US serviceman, and injuring over 200 in October 2002. Although the perpetrators have not been identified, the Philippines intelligence community suspects that the bombings were carried out by the al-Qaida affiliated Abu Sayyaf, a group that has suffered significantly as a result of post 9/11 US assistance to the Armed Forces of the Philippines. On October 28, a terrorist opened fire on Laurence Foley, a 60-year old US diplomat working in Jordan as an administrator for the US Agency for International Development (USAID).[24] Foley was shot seven times point blank in his chest while heading for his car parked in the garage of his home in Amman. The Shurafaa al-Urdun (The Honorables of Jordan), a suspected front for al-Qaida, claimed that Foley was killed in protest of US support for Israel and the "bloodshed in Iraq and Afghanistan."[25] The attack came just as a warning was issued in August 2002 by the US government according to which al-Qaida was planning to kidnap US citizens in Jordan.

Following the tradition of the Prophet Muhammad, who called for his enemies to convert to Islam before subduing them, al-Qaida launched multiple attacks in Kuwait, Yemen, and Bali, all in the second week of October 2002, only after appealing to his adversaries. Bin Laden said: "In the name of God, the

---

23 Analysis of the Latest Bombing Incident in Indonesia and Its Possible Connections with Al Qaida and Jemmah Islamiyah, National Intelligence Coordinating Agency, Philippines, October 2002.

24 USAID is a leading disaster relief agency engaged in agriculture, irrigation and humanitarian programs.

25 The same group had claimed responsibility for the killing of Israeli diamond merchant Yitzhak Snir, a man in his 50s who was slain near Foley's home on August 6, 2001. The group said the attack was in response to Israeli mistreatment of Palestinians. Israeli security officials suspected that two previous attacks launched against Israeli citizens in Jordan were also perpetrated by the same group. On December 5 2000, an unidentified gunman shot and slightly wounded Israeli diplomat Shlomo Razabi in the left foot as he was leaving an Amman store. On November 19 2000, Israeli diplomat Yoram Havivian was slightly wounded in the arm and the leg when a gunman fired on his vehicle.

merciful, the compassionate; a message to the American people; peace be upon those who follow the right path. I am an honest advisor to you. I urge you to seek the joy of life and the afterlife, and to rid yourself of your dry, miserable and spiritless materialistic life. I urge you to become Muslims, for Islam calls for the principle of 'There is no God but Allah' and for justice, and it forbids injustice and criminality. I also call on you to understand the lesson of the New York and Washington raids, which came in response to some of your previous crimes. The aggressor deserves punishment. However, those who follow the movement of the criminal gang at the White House, the agents of the Jews, who are preparing to attack and partition the Islamic World, without you disapproving of this, realize that you have not understood anything from the message of the two raids....We beseech Almighty God to provide us with His support. He is the protector and has the power to do so. Say: O People of the Book! Come to common terms between us and you: That we worship none but Allah; that we associate no partners with Him; that we erect not from among ourselves lords and patrons other than Allah. If then they turn back, say ye: Bear witness that we at least are Muslims bowing to Allah's will."[26]

To assess the statements of bin Laden and Zawahiri, the CIA approached the most senior al-Qaida leaders in US detention, Abu Zubaidah, former head of al-Qaida's external operations, and Ramzi bin Al Shibh, the chief logistics officer of the 9/11 operation. They interpreted with dead accuracy that bin Laden would not make such a statement unless the organization was "ready and able to carry out such attacks." According to Abu Zubaidah, "bin Laden's modus operandi consisted of reviewing operational plans, weighing the consequences of each, selecting targets, and finally releasing his message regarding an impending attack. The plan has been approved and the timing is now determined by the operatives and the local security situation."[27] They said that just as the prophet had urged his opponents to embrace Islam before

---

26 Osama bin Laden's two-minute audiotape broadcast marking the first anniversary of the US intervention in Afghanistan, Al Jazeera, Arab Satellite Television Station, Qatar, October 6, 2002.

27 Al-Qaida Declarations of Continued Attacks, CIA, Langley, October 2002, p. 1.

being subdued by his army, bin Laden was calling on his opponents to convert to Islam before attacking them. Although the tape was Koranically justify his course of action to his internal constituency.

Diffusion of Threat

Both the fanning out of al-Qaida cells and the launching of spectacular attacks have certainly made anti- and counter-terrorism initiatives difficult and complex. As terrorists are copycats, the direct and indirect influence of al-Qaida is reflected in the changing behavior of several groups. As terrorist groups closely guard their foreign linkages, it has often become difficult even for government intelligence agencies to identify the exact nature of their external relationships. While the Russian secret service is convinced of the al-Qaida-Chechen terrorist nexus, the Western press has demonstrated a grave reluctance to call Chechen groups that practice terrorism "terrorists."[28] On October 23 2002, 600 miles away from Moscow, 53 Chechen male and female suicide terrorists stormed the 1163 seat auditorium of Act II screening Nord-Ost (North East), a popular misical.[29] After booby-trapping the theatre containing 850 hostages, they demanded that Russian forces withdraw from Chechnya. The next day, they sent a video tape to Al Jazeera in which a hostage taker said: "I swear by God we are more keen on dying than you are keen on living.....each one of us is willing to sacrifice himself for the sake of God and the independence of Chechnya."[30] On October 26, after the terrorists began to execute their hostages, Spetsnaz commandos in the elite Alfa and Vympel anti-terror squads of the Federal Security Service rescued the hostages after dispersing sleeping gas through the ventilation system and holes bored underneath the auditorium. Of the 119 dead hostages, only two died of gun shot injuries—others perished from the gas, due to lack of timely

---

28 Valeria Korchagina, "Hostage-takers 'keen on dying.'" USA Today, October 25, 2002, p. 14 A. The article uses the term "rebels."

29 After the first Chechen war (December 1994-November 1996), Russian troops withdrew from Chechnya but returned in 1999 following a series of apartment bombings in Moscow that killed 300 Russians.

30 Chechen Tape, Al Jezeera, October 24, 2002.

medical care. The Moscow operation was conducted by 25-year-old Movsar Barayev, nephew of Arbi Barayev, the Chechen Islamist Special Unit leader who oversaw the beheading of four telecommunication workers from Britain and New Zealand in Chechnya in 1998.[31] The deputies of the Chechen rebel President Aslan Maskhadov were Shamil Basayev (the leader) and Ibn ul-Khattab (the military leader), and Majlis ul-Shura of the Mujahidin of Ichkeria and Dagestan respectively.[32] Khattab, at the time the commander of the Al Ansar Mujahidin (Islamic International Brigade) and a protégé of bin Laden, was assassinated by the Russian secret service on March 19, 2002. Movsar was close to Khattab, who remained a part of the al-Qaida network until his death.[33] Khattab was succeeded by Muhammad al Ghamdi, alias Abu Walid, the cousin of two 9/11 hijackers, the Ghamdi brothers, all from the Southern Saudi Province of Asir. The Moscow operation bore the primary three hallmarks of al-Qaida: (a) grandiose operations (2) suicide (3) targeting the heart, and (4) coordinated simultaneous attacks.

The second post-9/11 wave targeted Riyadh, Casablanca, Chechnya and Karachi in May 2003. Demonstrating that the group remains a resilient threat, al-Qaida coordinated the timing of its attack in Riyadh with the timings of the bombings perpetrated by its associated groups in North Africa, the Caucuses and in Asia. To compensate for the loss of significant personnel and physical infrastructure, al-Qaida relies on its associate groups to stage operations.

Despite the fact that it was being hunted by Saudi intelligence and law enforcement agencies, al-Qaida was able to plan, prepare and execute an operation in the heart of the Kingdom on May 12, 2003. In spite of both

---

31 Movsar's aunt Khava Barayev, 19, perpetrated a suicide attack killing two Russian soldiers at the Russian base at Alkhan-Yurt in June 2000.

32 Poisoned Letter Killed Chechen Commander Khattab, Kavkaz-Tsentr News Agency Website in Russian April 28, 2002.

33 Al Qaida's former Southeast Asian representative Umar Al Faruq's cell phone number 081-2802-7614 was in the phone memory of Ibn-ul-Khattab as well as the phone number of another Al Qaida leader Abu Talha alias Muhammad Abdallah Nasir Ubayd al Dusari arrested by the Kuwaitis. Tactical Interrogation Report, Umar Al Faruq, CIA, Langley, September 2002.

technical and human domestic and foreign intelligence, indicating that al-Qaida was in the final phases of an operation, Saudi authorities failed to detect and thwart the operation that destroyed three poorly protected foreign residential complexes in Riyadh at 23:25 on May 12, 2003. The triple suicide attacks claimed 34 victims in Al Hamra, Coroval, and Jedawal, including nine bombers, and injured 194 people. A fourth explosion detonated at the offices of Siyanco, a Saudi Maintenance Company and a venture between Frank E. Basil Inc of Washington and local Saudi Partners, but there were no casualties.

On May 16 in Morocco, suicide bombers attacked Casa de Espana, a Spanish social club, the Hotel Farah, a Jewish community center and cemetery, and a restaurant next to the Belgium consulate in Casablanca, all within 20 minutes. In addition to 12 bombers who perished in the raids, the attacks killed 27 and injured 100. Of the 14-man attack team, one failed suicide bomber was captured, and subsequently one bomber was arrested. The attacks in Saudi Arabia and Morocco bore the hallmarks of al-Qaida. Al-Qaida in Saudi Arabia and its associated group Assirat al-Moustaquim (The Straight Path) in Morocco perpetrated the coordinated simultaneous suicide attacks against Western and Jewish targets with the aim of inflicting maximum fatalities.

In Chechnya, Al Ansar Mujahidin, an associate group of al-Qaida, mounted suicide operations at Znamenskoye, killing 59 and injuring 200, also on May 12, and at Iliskhan-Yurt killing 18 and injuring 100 on May 14. The bombings in Chechnya were aimed at generating mass fatalities and fear—targeting offices and homes at Znamenskoye, the northern district of Nadterechny, and the assassination of Akhmad Kadyrov, the Chechen administration leader, near a shrine in Iliskhan-Yurt where 15,000 Muslims had gathered to mark the birth of Prophet Muhammad. An Ansar Mujahidin is led by Abu Walid, alias Muhammad al Ghamdi, the successor of Ibn Omar al Khattab, both Afghan veterans and protégés of Osama bin Laden.

In Pakistan, the Muslim United Army (MUA) simultaneously bombed 19 Shell and two Caltex gasoline stations in Nazimabad, Joharabad, SITE, Sharea Faisal and Gulshan-I-Iqbal, all in Southern Karachi between 4-5 a.m. on May 15. MUA is believed to be Lashkar-e-Jhangvi, an al-Qaida associated group in Pakistan. The improved explosive devices, weighing 200 grams and equipped with 15-minute timers, were planted by motorcyclists inside garbage cans near fuel pumps. The bombings damaged the Pakistani infrastructure owned by Anglo, Dutch and American companies and injured one customer, three station attendants and one security guard. To prevent such attacks, Pakistan had already increased security of various food chains—Pizza Hut, MacDonalds and KFC, but the group had selected its tactics and targets creatively. The bombing came to avenge Pakistan's hunt for al-Qaida and its associate members in Pakistan.

Middle East—Striking the Heartland

For those who believed that al-Qaida is dead, the attack in Riyadh on May 12, 2003 demonstrated that al-Qaida remains a significant threat in the coming months, if not years. Despite recurrent indications and warnings, including one issued by the CIA that "they are coming for you," the Saudis remained defiant, stating that "everything was under control."[34] Two weeks prior to the attack, it was very clear to both the American and the Saudi authorities that al-Qaida was in the final phases of launching an operation.

There were multiple indications and at least one warning the week preceding the attack. This included a US government warning pertaining to the likelihood of an attack in Saudi Arabia. Although the warning was not target specific, it was country specific. Under the no-double-standards policy, the US was mandated to issue all general and specific warnings to its citizens both at home and overseas in the public domain. On April 29, the US Embassy in Riyadh requested that Saudi authorities increase the security around the residential complexes. On May 1, the US State Department issued a travel warning requesting that private US citizens in Saudi Arabia consider departing and that non-essential travel by Americans be deferred. On May 6, nineteen members of al-Qaida escaped following a gunfight with the Saudi security forces. During the confrontation, demonstrating their willingness to kill and die,

---

34 George Tenant, CIA Director visited Riyadh a few weeks before the attack and apprised the House of al Saud of the impending threat. Interview, CIA officer, May 2003.

one member detonated a device and killed himself. The 19 had fought with Osama bin Laden in the Tora Bora battles in Afghanistan. They were the same members that launched the operation. One al-Qaida member surrendered and provided information about the al-Qaida organization in Saudi Arabia but disclosed nothing about the attack. The Saudis released the identities of the 19 wanted men, requesting the public's assistance. On May 7, a spokesman for al Qaida, Thabet bin Qais, stated that Osama bin Laden's forces were gearing up for a series of attacks. On May 7, the US Embassy in Riyadh appealed to the Saudi authorities to enhance the security of the residential complexes. On May 8, Saudi authorities seized 800 lbs of explosives, automatic weapons, grenades, ammunition, computers, communication equipment and money from both a house and a vehicle about a quarter of a mile from Jedawal, one of the complexes attacked subsequently. On May 10, the US Embassy in Riyadh again requested that the Saudi authorities increase the security of the residential complexes. The US Embassy specifically requested that the Saudi authorities provide additional protection for the Jedawal complex. On May 11, al-Qaida member Abu Mohammed Ablaj wrote to the London-based Al-Majalla magazine that the armed martyrdom squads were about to attack. "Besides targeting the heart of America, one of the strategic priorities now is to target and execute operations in the Gulf countries against allies of the United States," Ablaj wrote in an email the day before the attack.

Even prior to these indications, the intelligence reports suggested that Saudi Arabia was coming under increasing threat. Both the CIA and the FBI informed their Saudi counterparts, nearly a year prior to the attack, that Abdel Rahman Jabarah, a Canadian al-Qaida member of Kuwaiti origin, had entered the Kingdom. Muhammad al-Johani led the operation. Abdel Rahman, one of the bombing's organizers, was the elder brother of Muhammad Mansour Jabarah, a 21-year-old al-Qaida operative being held in US custody. After the thwarting of an al-Qaida campaign against US and Israeli diplomatic targets in Manila and the US, as well as British, Australian and Israeli diplomatic targets in Singapore in December 2001, its operations coordinator Muhammad Mansour fled to the Middle East. He was arrested in Oman in March 2002. Both the operations commander, Muhammad al-Johani, and the Canadian brothers worked under Khalid Sheikh Muhammad, the head of al-Qaida's Military Committee, and his successor and Deputy Tawfiq Attash, both of whom were arrested in Rawalpindi and Karachi, Pakistan in March, 2003. Al-Johani, who had left Saudi Arabia when he was 18, returned there with a forged passport in March 2003 to conduct the operation. Operating under the al-Qaida front of "The Mujahideen in the Peninsula," al Johani structured the organization so that it would be able to conduct attacks in the region starting with Saudi Arabia. Thirty-six hours after the attack, 'Al-Muwahhidun' (Those who Profess the Oneness of God), a front for al-Qaida, claimed responsibility for the attack. The new front was under the leadership of three fugitives—Ali bin Khudair Al-Khudair, Nasir bin Hamd Al-Fahd, and Ahmad bin Hamd Al-Khalid—and nineteen others who were wanted.

As the attack targeted Westerners, and it was the first attack against a Western target after the US intervened and occupied Iraq, it will be viewed with mix feelings within the Kingdom and the Middle East. The elite, who want to retain their power and status, will aspire to control the group. However, the suppression and repression of the al-Qaida brand Islamists are likely to generate a fresh wave of recruits and support for al-Qaida and its associated groups in the Gulf. While the Saudi over-reaction is likely to decrease the threat in the short term, it will increase Saudi public support for al-Qaida in the long term. Unless Saudi Arabia reforms the country's education system, Osama bin Laden, the popular hero of all Saudis who oppose the House of al Saud, will remain their symbol of resistance.

Outside of the Middle East, al-Qaida members are concentrated in the Horn of Africa, the Caucuses (Chechnya and Pankishi Gorge in Georgia), and in Asia. Africa, and especially the Horn, have always been the Achilles' heel of the international intelligence community. Intelligence on the Horn has improved since August 1998 but not appreciably. While based in Sudan (December 1991-May 1996), al-Qaida made significant inroads into the East African countries, and continues to operate in the Horn. While the Russian military has sustained heavy losses in Chechnya, the US Special Operations Forces working with the Georgian forces are conducting operations to clear the gorge. Several hundred US personnel based in Djibouti are engaged in activities in the Horn of Africa and Yemen. In addition to Afghanistan and Pakistan, al-Qaida elements have a presence throughout Asia. For instance, al-Qaida members regularly infiltrate Kashmir and Bangladesh in South Asia. In addition to the Middle East, when it comes to regions, the Horn of Africa and Southeast Asia present the greatest challenges. Even before the gravity of terrorism shifted from the Middle East to Asia in the early 1990s, the Middle Eastern groups were active in Southeast Asia.

Southeast Asia: a New Theatre

Of the two-dozen Islamist terrorist groups active in Southeast Asia, JI presents the greatest threat. There are about 400 al-Qaida-trained JI members in Southeast Asia. With the exception of Afghanistan and Pakistan, Southeast Asia is the home of the single largest concentration of al-Qaida-trained active members in any given region. The presence of 240 million Muslims, emerging democracies, corrupt governments, weak rulers, as well as the absence of security, all enable Southeast Asia to emerge as a new centre for al-Qaida activity. Historically, Southeast Asia has featured prominently in all al-Qaida operations including 9/11. Khalid Sheikh Muhammad, the head of the al-Qaida military committee, convened a meeting of 12 al-Qaida operatives in Kuala Lumpur from January 5-12, 2000 in order to coordinate both the USS Cole and the 9/11 operations. Immediately prior to 9/11, bin Laden dispatched the organization's key financier (a Kuwaiti of Canadian citizenship) Muhammad Mansour Jabarah, alias Sammy, to Malaysia to plan and prepare the attacks against US and Israeli diplomatic targets in Manila, Philippines. After visiting the embassies with al-Qaida suicide bomber Ahmed Sahagi, Jabarah concluded that "the attack on the US Embassy in Manila would have been much more difficult" and that "a plane would be needed to attack this building because the security was very tough."[35] Therefore, al-Qaida decided to shift the operation to Singapore where the "embassy is very close to the streets and did not have many barriers to prevent the

---

35 Information Received from Muhammad Mansour Jabarah, Federal Bureau of Investigations, US Department of Justice, August 21, 2002, p. 2.

attack."[36] Due to the difficulty in shipping the explosives to Singapore from the Philippines, Nurjaman Riduan Isamuddin, alias Hambali, a 36-year-old Indonesian serving both on the al-Qaida and JI Shura (Consultative) Councils, decided to cancel the Singapore operation involving the attacks against US, British, Australian and Israeli diplomatic targets—and choose "better" targets in the Philippines. The detection and disruption of the Singapore operation by Singapore's Internal Security Department led to the discovery of al-Qaida's JI regional network in December 2001. Although the Malaysian and the Philippine governments arrested JI members, Indonesia's President Megawatti Sukarnoputri was reluctant to follow suit, and as a result about 180 JI members moved to Indonesia and Thailand. In Southern Thailand, Hambali and Jabarah discussed bombings in "bars, cafes, or nightclubs frequented by Westerners in Thailand, Malaysia, Singapore, Philippines and Indonesia."[37] Although Hambali's original plan was to conduct a number of small bombings in line with the in-house capability and modus operandi of JI, the arrival of bomb-making experts and financing from al-Qaida enhanced JI's technical expertise, enabling it to conduct large-scale bombings.

The Moro Islamic Liberation Front (MILF), an associate group of al-Qaida, provided training to JI recruits in Mindanao, Philippines. After Camp Abu Bakar was overrun in April 2000, the MILF and JI established training camps in Poso and Sulawesi in Indonesia and in Balikpapan and Sampit in Kalimanthan.[38] Even after the resumption of the MILF-Manila government peace talks, MILF camps in Vietnam, Hudeibiya and the PA continue to provide facilities to hundreds of foreign nationals including Arab members of al-Qaida. The arrests of the Pakastani Muhammad Saad Iqbal Madni in Indonesia in January 2002, and of the Kuwaiti Omar Al Farook, alias Mahmoud bin Ahmed Assegaf (former leader of Camp Vietnam), in June of that year provided insight into MILF-JI linkages and future al-Qaida plans.[39] Omar

---

36 Ibid

37 Ibid.

38 Umar Faruq's Terrorist Activities in Indonesia, BIN, Jakarta, June 2002, p. 2.

39 Ibid, p. 2.

Al Farook also divulged attack plans and information regarding monetary transfers, including US$ 73,000 from Sheikh Abu Abdallah Al Emarati of Saudi Arabia to Abu Bakar Bashir in Indonesia for the purchase of explosives. An Indonesian intelligence report states: "In the absence of an Internal Security Act, it is almost impossible for the Indonesian government to take legal action against anybody involved in al-Qaida unless he has committed a crime. Therefore, Farook was deported on immigration grounds and due to the illegal acquisition of documents. He was arrested on June 5 [2002]. On June 8 [2002], he was deported to the US Air Force base in Baghram, Afghanistan."[40] The JI's spiritual, ideological and political leader is Abu Bakar Bashir (who also played an operational role). Hambali is the operational commander of JI and al-Qaida in Southeast Asia. Unlike Indonesia and Thailand, which have denied the existence of a terrorist network, the Philippines have determinedly fought terrorism. However, it lacks the resources of the US, the support of European governments, and the cooperation of its neighbours, and as a result is forced to negotiate even with the MILF, a group that has refrained from condemning bin Laden and al-Qaida.

The absence of a zero tolerance terrorism policy in the region and beyond facilitated the spawning and sustenance of a robust terrorist support and operational network. After the JI network was discovered in December 2001, Indonesia permitted the continued operation of a fully-fledged JI infrastructure. This remained the case despite the Al Farook and Jabarah debriefings indicating the continued exploitation of Indonesia and Thailand by JI and al-Qaida. These, as well as neighboring governments, failed to engage in sustained targeting of terrorist operatives and assets. Despite the provision of strategic information by the US intelligence community, including the threat to bomb "bars, cafes, or nightclubs," regional governments failed to enhance the ground, contact or tactical intelligence with technical and human source penetration. The Australian government should have invested sufficient

---

40 Although BIN headed by A.M. Hendropriyono targeted Al Qaida cells, the Indonesian government was reluctant to target JI and its associated Majlis Mujahidin Indonesia (MMI: Mujahidin Council of Indonesia) headed by Abu Bakar Bashir, and Lashkar Jundullah headed by Agus Dwikarna.

resources inside its immediate neighbourhood to dampen Islamism, and could have used the JI infrastructure in Perth, Sydney, Melbourne and Adelaide to penetrate the network. Despite the participation of a dozen Australian citizens and residents in JI and al-Qaida training camps from Mindanao, Philippines to Afghanistan,[41] the government and operational agencies did not believe that the threat was "significant" until Bali.[42]

Liberal Democracies: North America, Europe, Australia

An examination of terrorist support and operational infrastructure worldwide reveals that liberal democracies offer ideal conditions for foreign terrorist groups to establish their support networks in the West. In order for terrorism to flourish, two prerequisites are needed; terrorists who conduct attacks and non-terrorists who provide support. To defeat terrorism, both of these categories must be targeted. During the past two decades, Asian, Middle Eastern and Latin American terrorist groups have established open offices or secret cells for disseminating propaganda, raising funds and specialized training, as well as procuring and transporting supplies in the West. For instance, Australia became the home of several foreign terrorist groups; the Palestinian Hamas, Lebanese Hizballah, Chechen mujahidin, the Kurdish Workers Party (Turkey), Euzkadi Ta Askatasuna (Spain), the Liberation Tigers of Tamil Eelam (Sri Lanka), Babbar Khalsa International (India) and International Sikh Youth Federation (India), as well as dissident factions of the Irish Republican Army. The foreign terrorist groups disseminate terrorist propaganda, recruit, raise funds, procure and transport technologies from the West to perpetrate terrorism elsewhere. As these groups did not pose a direct and an immediate threat to host countries, Western security and intelligence agencies monitored these groups without disrupting their propaganda, fund raising, procurement and transportation infrastructure. As a result, several terrorists, their supporters and sympathizers, infiltrated Western society and

---

41 Debriefing of John Walker Lindh, Virginia, US, July 25, 2002.

42 Margo O'Neill, Lateline, Australian Broadcasting Corporation, October 9, 2002.
    Australian government saw no significant threat to Australia or to its interests.

governments. These foreign terrorist groups diverted the resources raised in the West to attack target countries in the global south.

In addition to establishing al-Qaida cells, the group also co-opted the leaderships of two European networks. As a result, both Takfir Wal Hijra and GSPC in Europe, and to a lesser extent in North America, present a significant threat to Western security. These two networks are fed by migrants from North Africa and are ideologically fuelled by the developments in the lands of jihad, particularly their home countries. Just as Europe witnessed a spill-over of terrorism from the Middle East, the developments in Southeast Asia have increased the threat to Australia and New Zealand and their interests overseas. Australia has been an al-Qaida target since 1999, but certain events have increased the threat to that country since 2000, such as Australia's high profile participation in the US-led, anti-terrorist campaign in Afghanistan in October 2001 followed by the angry reaction of Australian Muslims, and bin Laden's claim in early November 2001 that Australia had conspired and led a crusade against the Islamic nation to dismember East Timor in November 2001, etc. A grenade was lobbed from a motorbike into the garden of the Australian International School in Jakarta in November 2001; large firecrackers were hurled into the Australian Embassy in Jakarta also in November 2001; an Arab al-Qaida suicide bomber in an explosives-laden truck planned to destroy the Australian High Commission in Singapore in early 2002.[43] Interrogations of al-Qaida and Taliban detainees and prisoners in Afghanistan, Pakistan, Camp Delta and the US revealed that Australian Muslims who had trained in Camp Al Farooq in Afghanistan and elsewhere were instructed to conduct terrorist operations against Australian targets.

---

43 Despite the fact that a JI surveillance video of the Australian target was recovered in the residence of the late Al Qaida military commander Muhammad Atef, alias Abu Hafs in Afghanistan, the Australian government did not take the threat seriously – some officials believed that Al Qaida/JI had included the Australian High Commission in the target list because it was next to the US Embassy. Even in March 2002, some Australian intelligence officials who participated in a counter-terrorism meeting organised by the Institute for Defense and Strategic Studies in Singapore disbelieved that JI was under Al Qaida control.

Before al-Qaida targeted Australians overseas, al-Qaida established a support network in Australia using its Southeast Asian arm—JI. Furthermore, JI penetration of local Muslim groups led to a significant generation of propaganda in Australia aimed at politicizing and radicalizing Australian Muslims. Sungkar spoke of the "obligation of jihad within the framework of aiming to resurrect dawlah islamiyyah" by applying the strategies of faith and its expression in word and action and jihad.[44] He added: "In this, quwwaatul musallaha or military strength is essential."[45] The JI leaders offered Indonesian Muslims two choices: "Life in a nation based upon the Koran and the Sunnah, or death while striving to implement, in their entirety, laws based on the Koran and the Sunnah."[46] Bin Laden gave an exclusive interview to his supporters in Australia that was published on a website in Australia. JI also raised funds in Australia and money was transferred from Australia, first to JI Malaysia and then with the disruption of the JI network in Malaysia, to JI Indonesia.[47] Furthermore, Australia features prominently in the JI regional structure. The JI network in the Asia-Pacific is divided into four geographical regions, which include Australia. JI's Area 4 or Mantiqi 4 (M4) covers Irian Jaya and Australia. As such, Australia has no option but to work jointly with the Southeast Asian countries to detect, disrupt, demote and destroy the JI organization. Its failure to do so will result in further attacks both in Australia and in its vicinity.

Another reason for the growing terror threat in Australia is that several terrorist groups in its immediate area—notably in the Philippines, Indonesia and Malaysia—have stepped up their activities at home and abroad. In addition, half a dozen groups linked to al-Qaida perceive Australia as an enemy. With the aim of strengthening security in the Asia-Pacific, Australia and the Southeast Asian region must improve cooperation. Up until Bali, there was definitely a very poor understanding of the threat to Australia. The Australian

---

44 Nida'ul Islam (Call to Islam), The Islamic Youth Movement Magazine, Sydney, February-March 1997

45 Ibid.

46 "The latest Indonesian crisis: causes and solutions," JI Political Manifesto, May 1998.

47 Debriefing of JI members, September-October 2002.

malaise stems from inadequate education regarding the Asia-Pacific region, as well as a poor understanding of the culture, politics and economics of its neighbours.[48] Even when you factor in a serious transnational terrorist threat, it seems that the 'it'll be alright' or 'it can't happen to us' attitude continues to prevail.[49] In the task that lies ahead, Australia lacks expertise and capacity, but it undoubtedly requires a shift of thinking on how its finite resources should be deployed. As a technologically advanced country with significant economic, political, diplomatic and military abilities Australia could also assist countries in Southeast Asia, especially Indonesia, to improve counter-terrorism capabilities. Australia can make a significant contribution to the ensuing criminal investigation by assisting Indonesia. Australia should adopt a leadership role in this campaign, in the region as a whole and especially with its Southeast Asian allies, in order to urge Indonesia to take action. Previous tragic events could encourage a rapid maturation of cooperation in the region, spurred on by Australia.

To meet the current threat, the Australian Security Intelligence Organization (ASIO), its counter-intelligence and anti-terrorist agency, the Australian Security and Intelligence Service (ASIS), and its overseas intelligence service, all need to double their efforts without losing quality and resources to operate effectively and efficiently. In order to improve security in Australia and New Zealand, Australian agencies must work closely with their New Zealand counterparts.

Afghanistan-Pakistan-Iran

In the aftermath of the US intervention in Afghanistan in October 2001, Osama bin Laden requested the bulk of the al-Qaida members to travel to their home countries and await instructions. Those who had come to the adverse attention of their home security and intelligence agencies were asked to remain in Pakistan. Al-Qaida's operational leaders Abu Zubaidah and Khalid

---

48 Interview, Jeff Pentrose, Former Director, Australian Federal Police Intelligence, October 2002

49 Ibid.

Sheikh Muhammad relocated to Pakistan and coordinated the global terrorist campaign until their arrests in March 2002 and May 2003 respectively. After the arrest of Khalid Sheikh Muhammad's successor Tawfiq bin Attash, Osama bin Laden appointed his Chief of Security Seif Al-'Adel, the new operations chief in April 2003. The May 2003 operations were executed by Seif Al-'Adel, a former officer of the Egyptian military, and thereafter a member of the Egyptian Islamic Jihad. After fighting against the Soviet Army, he joined al-Qaida and then trained with the Hizballah in Southern Lebanon. In the Riyadh operation, Seif Al-'Adel joined forces with another senior member, Abu Khaled, and Osama bin Laden's son, Sa'ad bin Laden, a bodyguard of the al-Qaida leader. Although the extent of Iranian sponsorship is unclear, the operational leadership that coordinated the Riyadh bombing and dispatched experts to Casablanca, Morocco in order to advise Assirat al-Moustaquim was located in Iran. Due to the loss of a large number of al-Qaida leaders and operatives in Pakistan, al-Qaida is increasingly looking to Iran. The Iraqi Islamist group Ansar al-Islami, another al-Qaida associate group, also operates on the Iran-Iraq border.

The international community has gravely neglected to rebuild Afghanistan and transform the war-ravaged country into a modern, 21st century state. Al-Qaida has resurrected itself in Afghanistan by working with Mullah Omar's Taliban and Gulbaddin Hekmatiyar's Hezbi-e-islami. Similarly, al-Qaida continues to work with Sipai Sahaba, Lashkar-e-Jenghvi, Lashkar-e-Toiba, Jayash-e-Mohommad, Harakart-ul-Mujahidin and a number of other Pakistani groups. With US security forces and the intelligence community targeting al-Qaida's nerve centre in Afghanistan-Pakistan, al-Qaida will decentralize even further. While its organizers of attacks will remain in Pakistan and its immediate vicinity, its operatives will travel back and forth coordinating with al-Qaida nodes in the south. To make its presence felt, al-Qaida will increasingly rely on its global terrorist network of like-minded groups in Southeast Asia, South Asia, the Horn of Africa, the Middle East, and the Caucuses to strike out at its enemies. Already attacks launched in Kenya, Indonesia, India, Pakistan, Kuwait and Yemen seek to compensate for the loss and lack of space and opportunity previously experienced in Afghanistan. With the transfer of terrorist technology and expertise from the centre to the periphery, the attacks perpetrated by al-Qaida's associated groups will pose a threat as great as al-Qaida.

Although al-Qaida is waging a universal jihad, the influence of al-Qaida on Muslim separatist groups active in their own territories is growing. This constitutes a worrying trend, as Islamists tend to "hijack" the resources of the ethno-nationalists. There is very little governments can do to arrest this trend. Whether it is in the Moroland in the Philippines, Aceh in Indonesia, Pattini in Thailand, Kashmir in India-Pakistan, or Chechnya in Russia, Muslim secessionist conflicts have been penetrated by Islamist groups to varying degrees. Either by emulation or direct contact, factions, splinters and main groups of the separatist category are learning from al-Qaida tactics, techniques and styles. Al-Qaida did not frequently engage in kidnapping, hostage-taking or assassination, but its camps in Afghanistan and elsewhere taught these tactics to several tens of thousands of activists.[50] Even before 9/11, there was indication that al-Qaida had been attempting to develop alliances with non-Islamist Muslim groups. Rabitat-ul Mujahidin is an alliance of Islamist and Muslim separatist groups from the Philippines, Indonesia, Malaysia, Myanmar and Thailand.[51] Thailand, particularly Bangkok and the Narathiwat Province, provide a safe haven for Jemmah Islamiyah. This country serves as the home base for a number of other groups including The Pattani United Liberation Organization (PULO) (formed in 1967), The New PULO (formed in 1995), The Barisan Revolusi Nasional Malayu Pattani (BRN) (formed in 1960), Gerakan Mujahideen Islam Pattani (GMIP) (formed in 1986), and Bersatu (Unity) formed in 1997.[52] Some of the GMIP members, such as Wae

---

50 The author reviewed over 200 tapes, including training tapes recovered by CNN's Nic Robertson from Al Qaida's registry in Afghanistan, CNN Centre, Atlanta, August-September 2002.

51 The second meeting of the Rabitat-ul Mujahidin held in Kuala Lumpur, Malaysia and presided by the JI leader Abu Bakar Basyir in mid-2000, included both Islamists and separatist leaders—Agus Dwikarna from Sulawesi, Tenku Idris from Aceh, Ibrahim Maidin from Singapore, Abdul Fatah from Thailand, Nik Adli Abdul Aziz from Malaysia, and representatives from Myanmar and the Egyptian Islamic Jihad. Interview, intelligence official, Department of the Prime Minister, Malaysia, November 2002.

52 Tony Davis, "The Complexities of Unrest in Southern Thailand," Jane's Intelligence Review, Volume 14 Number 9, September 2002. p. 17.

Ka Raeh, trained in Afghanistan and fought for al-Qaida.[53] Despite the Thai government's successes in bringing secessionist violence to an end in the 1980s, there has been a revival since 2001. On October 29 2002, Southern Thailand was the site of a series of arson incidents and explosions. Five schools were set on fire in Songkhla Province and bombs damaged both My Garden Hotel and a Buddhist temple in the neighboring Pattani Province in 2001. Since April 2001, about two-dozen law enforcement officers have been killed in southern Thailand but the authorities in Bangkok have attributed the violence to crime rather than terrorist activity. After Bali, the threat to popular tourist destinations, including Pukhet and Pataya in Thailand, has increased. Furthermore, activity of the al-Qaida network in Thailand, from which two of the 9/11 hijackers were launched following a meeting held in Malaysia in January 2000, continues undisrupted. After living in denial for one and a half years, Thailand was forced to arrest Thai JI members in June 2003, following the apprehension of a Singaporean JI member in Bangkok. As a result, an attack being planned by JI Thailand against diplomatic targets in Bangkok and two tourist resorts was thwarted.

Ideological Threat

More than an organization, the ideology of al-Qaida remains a resilient threat. Although al-Qaida can still mount operations, due to the intensified pressure, the organization will eventually be relegated to an ideology. As al-Qaida increasingly depends on like-minded groups to conduct attacks, other Islamist groups will become similar to al-Qaida. For instance, Mas Salamat Kasthari, Chief of the Singapore Jemmah Islamiyah (JI), was planning to hijack an Aerofloat plane from Bangkok and crash it into the Changi International Airport in Singapore in 2002. The tactic of using an air vehicle as a weapon was clearly an al-Qaida invention. When asked by his interrogators why he had chosen to hijack an Aerofloat plane, he responded that JI had decided to teach Russia a lesson for killing civilians in Chechnya. Furthermore, the modus operandi used by the same group in the mass killing of 202 civilians in Bali was not characteristically Southeast Asian. Southeast Asia had never witnessed a mass fatality terrorist attack before. Likewise, the JI attack in Bali

---

53 Ibid. p. 17.

was the first suicide attack to be perpetrated by a Southeast Asian terrorist.[54] During the past decade, JI and other associated Islamist groups have been substantially influenced by al-Qaida.

Traditionally, al-Qaida, with its better trained, more experienced and highly committed operatives, has aspired to attack more difficult targets, particularly ones with strategic value, while leaving the easier and tactical targets to its associated groups. With al-Qaida decentralizing, its operatives are working closely at a tactical level with other groups. As a result, the lethality of the attacks conducted by the associate groups of al-Qaida is increasing. As Bali in 2002 and Casablanca in 2003 demonstrated, the attacks perpetrated by the associate groups of al-Qaida can be as lethal as the attacks launched by the parent group itself. With attacks perpetrated by al-Qaida's associated groups posing as great a threat as al-Qaida's activities, the theatre of war will expand. Government security and intelligence agencies will be forced to monitor the technologies, tactics and techniques of a wide range of groups.

Although the US is under severe pressure to withdraw from Saudi Arabia, the former will prefer to remain in the Kingdom because withdrawal in the aftermath of the recent attack will be interpreted as defeat in the eyes of its opponents. Nonetheless, US visibility in the Middle East, US assistance to Israel and the continued US presence in Iraq will all trigger wide-ranging reactions from the Islamists, both terrorist groups and political parties. In the aftermath of the intervention of the US, its allies, and the Coalition in Afghanistan on October 7, 2001, Iraq represents an attractive base for al-Qaida. The Islamists desperately need a new theater to produce psychologically and physically war-trained Islamists.

Successes and Failures

Although branded a "War against Terrorism" by the US, the battle is against a radical ideology producing Muslim youth willing to kill and die, as well

---

54 Iqbal, a JI member, detonated a backpack of explosives that he carried into Paddy's Bar in Bali.

as wealthy Muslims willing to provide support and suffer incarceration. For the al-Qaida umbrella—the World Islamic Front for Jihad Against the Jews and the Crusaders—the struggle is against a civilization. In reality, it is a battle between the vast majority of progressive Muslims and the miniscule percentage of radical Muslims. It is not a clash of civilizations but a clash among civilizations—a contest that must essentially be fought within the Muslim world. While the immediate (1-2 years) consequences are apparent, the mid- (5 years) and long-term (10 years) consequences of militarily engaging in a primarily ideological campaign are yet to be seen. Everything indicates that Islamism—whether it is in Turkey, Pakistan, Malaysia, or in Indonesia—is shifting from the periphery to the centre. US intervention in Iraq has provided the ideological fuel prolonging the strength, size and life of Islamist political parties and terrorist groups.

The greatest failure of the US-led coalition is its inability to neutralize the core leadership of both al-Qaida and the Islamic Movement of the Taliban. While preparations for protracted guerrilla operations against the coalition forces inside Afghanistan are coordinated by Taliban leader Mullah Mohommad Omar, terrorist operations worldwide, including in Afghanistan, are coordinated by Osama bin Laden and his deputy, principal strategist and designated successor Dr Ayman Zawahiri. Multiple sources, including the CIA, indicate that both bin Laden and al-Zawahiri are alive.[55] Furthermore, Zawahiri actually refers to suicide attacks on the oldest North African Jewish synagogue in Djerba, Tunisia, killing 21, including 14 German tourists on April 11 2002, and the killing of 14 people, including 11 French naval technicians working on the submarine project outside the Sheraton Hotel in Karachi, Pakistan, on May 9, 2002. He states, "Thank God, America could not reach the leaders of al-Qaida and Taliban, including Mullah Muhammad Omar and Shayak Osama bin Laden, who enjoy good health and, alongside the rest of the patient mujahidin, are managing the battle against the US crusader raid on Afghanistan"[56] Members of the former Army of the Islamic Emirate Afghanistan, who are

---

55 Al-Qa'ida Declarations of Continued Attacks, CIA, Langley, October 2002, p. 1.

56 Ayman Al Zawahiri's question and answer with an unidentified reporter, Al Jazeera, October 8, 2002.

loyal to Mullah Omar and the surviving members of al-Qaida's 055 Brigade, support, or are engaged in, guerrilla and terrorist operations against the US-led coalition, both inside and outside Afghanistan respectively. Mullah Omar is building a clandestine network slowly but steadily in Afghanistan, utilizing its vast and porous borders to wage a protracted campaign of sustained urban warfare. Bin Laden and Zawahiri are developing targets overseas, especially soft targets with a twin focus on population centers and economic facilities.

Change of Mindest

To make things difficult for its enemies, al-Qaida has constantly innovated its military tactics, financial methods and propaganda techniques in the past year. Al-Qaida—which focused on strategic targets prior to 9/11—is now operating across the entire spectrum, targeting both strategic and tactical targets. Although in the first four months after 9/11, the West seized terrorist funds amounting to US$ 150 million, with the shifting of al-Qaida's financial practices, only about $10 million has been seized. With the targeting of the above-ground open banking system, the underground, unregulated banking network (hawala) has expanded. With mosques, madrasas, charities and community centers that disseminate Islamist propaganda coming under threat, al-Qaida is increasingly relying on the Internet. As al-Qaida is a learning organization, involved in an ongoing struggle against law enforcement, security and intelligence, it must be goal-oriented rather than rule-oriented.

While the terrorists are endeavoring to adapt to the threat posed by government law enforcement authorities as well as government security and intelligence agencies, the latter are increasing their human and technical source penetration. Capabilities vis-à-vis terrorist tracking, as well as the preemption and disruption of terrorist operations are increasing. For instance, an al-Qaida team traveling in their vehicle in Yemen's northern Province of Marib was attacked by a Hellfire missile launched from a CIA-controlled, unmanned Predator drone on November 4, 2002. Ali Senyan al-Harthi, alias Qaed Senyan al-Harthi alias Abu Ali, the mastermind behind the USS Cole operation and a key al-Qaida leader in the region was killed in the attack. To meet the current threat, the Pentagon has enhanced its intelligence capabilities and the CIA has increased its paramilitary capabilities. In the foreseeable future, human intelligence and covert strike forces will remain at the heart of the combat against secret and highly motivated organizations like al-Qaida. It is critical for the US to increase the sharing of intelligence, especially with its Middle Eastern and Asian counterparts. Traditionally, the US has been averse to sharing high-grade intelligence, particularly source-based intelligence, with the Muslim World. This policy has changed to a certain extent since 9/11, but not adequately.

If al-Qaida is to be defeated, a change in thinking regarding the US-led "War on Terrorism" is paramount. Despite the US-led coalition campaign worldwide, the al-Qaida alliance—the World Islamic Front for Jihad Against the Jews and Crusaders—has managed to repair the damage to its support and operational infrastructure. As no serious international effort has been made to counter the Islamist ideology (i.e., the belief that "every Muslim's duty is to wage jihad"), the robust Islamist milieu is providing recruits and financial support for Islamist groups worldwide to replenish their human losses and material wastage. Today, two to four al-Qaida and Taliban members may be captured or killed each week in Afghanistan, but at the end of that week, the Islamists are successful in attracting a dozen recruits as members, collaborators, supporters and sympathizers.[57] To put it crudely, the production rate of Islamists is greater than the rate of their disappearance due to demise or capture. The powerful message that al-Qaida is not Koranic but heretical has not been integrated within the counter-terrorism toolbox. Thus, there is overwhelming popular support for the al-Qaida model of Islam among the politicized and radicalized Muslims. As no effort is made to counter or dilute the extremist ideology, even if pursued single-mindedly and unrelentingly, the military campaign against al-Qaida is likely to take decades. The "deep reservoir of hatred and desire for revenge"[58] will thrive, unless the US can start to think beyond the counter-terrorist, military and financial dimensions.

---

57 Interviews, US military and intelligence officials, Washington DC, October 29-November 1, 2002.

58 Brian Michael Jenkins. Countering Al Qaida: An Appreciation of the Situation and Suggestions for Strategy, RAND, 2002

The international community must seek to build a zero tolerance level for terrorist support activity. The tragedies of 9/11, Bali, Moscow, Riyadh, Casablanca and several other attacks demonstrate that contemporary terrorists are indiscriminate. As terrorists do not recognize or respect ethnicity, religion or national borders, terrorism should be fought irrespective of location. There can be no appeasement with those who seek to advance their political aims and objectives through the use of violence. As in the case of Indonesia, countries that condone, tolerate or fail to take tough action against terrorism will be hurt by it. Not only countries in the Southern Hemisphere have been complacent vis-à-vis the fight against terrorism, but countries in the North as well. As stated earlier, within four months of 9/11, Western governments froze US$150 million worth of terrorist money in Europe and North America. This is indicative of the magnitude of terrorist wealth in liberal democracies. Although al-Qaida's support network has suffered in the US, its propaganda, recruitment and fundraising activities are still continuing in Europe. Despite counter efforts, segments of Muslims in the migrant communities of North America, Western Europe and Australia, and territorial communities in the Middle East and Asia, continue to provide support to al-Qaida and other Islamist groups. As Europe has not suffered a large-scale attack, Europeans do not perceive al-Qaida as a great threat. As a result, Islamist support activities are continuing in Western Europe. With the intensified threat, both governments and their publics that do not take threat information seriously are bound to suffer.

Managing the Threat

Al-Qaida has had a head start of ten years. Until one month after US diplomatic targets in East Africa were destroyed by al-Qaida in August 1998, the US intelligence community did even not know the correct name of Osama bin Laden's group.[59] However, during the past two years, the US intelligence

---

59 None of the CIA documents prior to August 1998 refers to Osama Bin Laden's organization as Al Qaida. It refers to the group as the UBL or OBL network and as Islamic Army. Furthermore, the 1997 US list of designated foreign terrorist groups makes no mention of Al-Qaida."

community's perception of its principal enemy—al-Qaida—has grown dramatically. The tragedy of 9/11 has empowered the CIA's Counter Terrorism Center to develop the much-needed organization, and more importantly, the mindset to hunt al-Qaida. Largely due to detainee debriefings, the West now understands the threat it faces far better than ever before. The US government, especially its security and intelligence community, has learnt at a remarkable pace. There is a marked improvement in collection and analysis both by the CIA and the FBI. For instance, immediately before the Yemeni, Kuwaiti, and Bali attacks, the CIA and FBI alerted friendly counterpart agencies and the US State Department issued worldwide alerts. The West, together with its Middle Eastern and Asian allies, seriously started fighting al-Qaida only after 9/11 and al-Qaida has suffered gravely in consequence. The global strategy of the West to meet the global threat posed by al-Qaida is taking shape slowly but steadily. Just as it contained the Soviet threat in the second half of the 20th century, so it will develop the organization and a doctrine to contain the Islamist threat. With sustained efforts to target the core and penultimate leadership, it is very likely that the al-Qaida top echelon of Osama bin Laden and Dr Ayman Al Zawahiri, and even the Taliban leader Mullah Omar, will be captured or more likely killed. Nonetheless, Islamist terrorism will outlive al-Qaida and Islamism as an ideology will persist in the foreseeable future.

The global war against terrorism will be carried out by the West and Japan —the rich and influential nations with the greatest staying power. With the diffusion of the terrorist threat, the US political, military, economic and diplomatic presence will grow and its influence will expand globally in the months and years ahead.[60] It is a long battle, and it will have to be waged on all fronts by multiple actors across many countries. To ensure the success of the campaign, the international community must remain focused on targeting al-Qaida and committed to rebuilding Afghanistan and Pakistan, and now Iraq. Western nations must move beyond rhetoric into concrete action, pour in resources, and build modern, model nation-states for the Muslim

---

60 In addition to the rise of Islamism, another factor that is driving an increased US presence worldwide is the reemergence of the People's Republic of China and US efforts to contain the next superpower.

world in these countries. Protecting Karzai of Afghanistan and Musharaff of Pakistan—the world's most threatened leaders—is paramount. Several attempts by al-Qaida and its associated groups to assassinate these leaders have been thwarted. International assistance for their regimes, by means of politically and economically developing their countries and investing in their publics, is the key to challenging the Islamists who continuously appeal to the politically and economically marginalized.

On the eve of the US intervention in Afghanistan, Osama bin Laden correctly stated that the fight has moved beyond al-Qaida. Al-Qaida's propaganda war since 9/11, especially following the US intervention in Iraq, has escalated many times over. With al-Qaida and pro-al-Qaida websites proliferating—many of them operationally unconnected but ideologically linked to al-Qaida—support for al-Qaida's ideology is slowly growing. Support for Islamism will grow even further if the US intervenes in Iraq. The world has recently witnessed several isolated terrorist incidents carried out by perpetrators influenced by terrorist propaganda. For instance, the Egyptian Hesham Muhammad Hadayet walked up to the El Al counter at Los Angeles International Airport and shot two people dead on America's Independence Day on July 4, 2002.[61] There were arrests worldwide, including in the heart of Europe, of several politicized and radicalized Muslims who provided funds or were preparing terrorist attacks. Osman Petmezci, a 24-year-old Turkish national, and his American fiancée Astrid Eyzaguirre, 23, were preparing to attack the US Army's European Headquarters in Heidelberg when they were arrested by the German authorities on September 5, 2002.[62] Inside the couple's third-floor apartment, police found 130 kilograms of chemicals used in bomb-making, five pipe bombs, a bomb-making manual, detonators and a picture of bin Laden. German authorities believe that the "couple was acting alone, despite their declared admiration for Osama bin Laden and common convictions, including a hatred for the Jews."[63] There are several similar unreported or

---

61 Shooting at Los Angeles International Airport Kills Two, Injures Others on July 4, FBI Press Release, Los Angeles Field Office, July 5, 2002.

62 Tony Czuczka, Germans had indications about a suspected bomb plot against the US, Associated Press, September 8, 2002.

63 Ibid

under-reported terrorist attacks. For instance, a US helicopter carrying US oil company employees was attacked after taking off from Yemen's San'a Airport, injuring two persons on November 3, 2002. With the steadfast erosion of al-Qaida personnel and its physical infrastructure, al-Qaida can become a state-of-mind, spawning both individual terrorists and successor terrorist organizations. To avoid this real danger, the ideological response to al-Qaida and Islamism as a doctrine must not be delegated a secondary role.

In order to win the campaign, the fight against radical Islam should not be confused with the Muslim world, which constitutes one fifth of humanity or 1.44 billion people.[64] It is not a clash of civilization but a clash among civilizations. It is a battle waged between the progressive Muslims and the radical Muslims. Only a miniscule percentage of the Muslim public actively supports terrorism.[65] The vast majority of Muslims have suffered as a result of political violence unleashed by a small group of power hungry leaders cloaked in the garb of religion. If the battle is to be won, efforts must be made to protect the moderate Muslims from virulent ideologies propagated by Mullahs of the al-Qaida brand of Islam. With the threat of Islamism rising, the efforts of progressive Muslim leaders both within and outside their governments, and especially within non-governmental organizations, must be boosted. These efforts should entail the warmest relations between Western governmental and non-governmental leaders and their Middle Eastern or Asian counterparts, and advocate open diplomacy where governments communicate directly with the public, even with publics across borders.[66] Despite the oil boom, the failure of Arab leaders to invest in their citizens has increased both the ideological appeal and the welfare programs of terrorist groups. The Arab regimes must take the blame for their failure to build modern education systems, create new

---

64 For statistics, US Centre for World Mission 2002 Report.

65 Husain Haqqani, "The Gospel of Jihad," Foreign Policy, September-October, 2002, p. 74.

66 The perception that the Indonesian military was behind the Bali bombing found resonance in Indonesia because the US government only engaged the Indonesian government and not the public. While strengthening government-to-government cooperation, it is also necessary to engage the public in a dialogue and keep them informed of the active presence of an Al Qaida-JI network in Indonesia.

jobs, and develop a quality of life for their people. The Arab world's habit of blaming the West for its ills and more importantly its reluctance to counter anti-Western rhetoric makes Western public diplomacy there even more vital. To counter Al Jazeera, a CNN, BBC or CBS Arab satellite television station can serve as a central tool to correct and fashion the traditional Middle Eastern view of the West. Instead of shying away, the West must engage the Middle East to develop transparency and accountability.[67] Furthermore, joint prophylactic measures—greater investment in political, socio-economic reform particularly in the areas of education and welfare—by the West and working together with the Muslim World are likely to reduce support for terrorism in the long term.[68] Failure to develop a multi-pronged, multi-dimensional, multi-agency and multinational response to al-Qaida and its associate groups will perpetuate the threat, and even cause its escalation.

---

67 For instance, charities should not be permitted to raise funds or transfer funds unless and
    until the end-user has been verified and validated.
68 Marina Ottaway, "Nation Building," Foreign Policy, September-October 2002, pp. 16-24.

Hizballah's Global Reach

Matthew Levitt

Senior Fellow, Washington Institute for Near East Policy, USA

An examination of Hizballah's international terrorist activity, that is its international presence and operations outside the Levant, not only illuminates the group's proactive and ongoing terror activities, but also provides a useful case study of a terrorist group of global reach.

Global Reach and Cross-group Pollination

Though the term has yet to be officially defined, "global reach" has nonetheless become the yardstick for determining whether or not a terrorist group warrants inclusion in the post-9/11 war on terrorism. Even within the "global reach" designation there exists an unstated spectrum of priorities. For example, al Qaida is legitimately going to receive more attention and resources than ETA in Spain or FARC in Colombia, even though both those regional terrorist groups are engaged in terrorist activity and are known for their links to other international terrorist groups and state sponsors.

A useful tool for the development of a more accurate barometer for gauging the extent of a group's global reach, and therefore its prioritization as a potential target in the war on terror, is the perception of the matrix of relationships between terrorist operatives, groups, fronts, and state sponsors. To be sure, these relationships are what make the threat of international terrorism so acute today, just as they constituted the single most critical factor in facilitating the success of the devastating attacks on September 11, 2001.

Indeed, while terrorist groups remain the central structural unit in international terrorism, I believe that the relationships between individual terrorists affiliated with different groups are even more important. This crossover and pollination facilitates cooperation among groups—if not operational, then certainly logistical and financial support. Such links exist even between groups that do not share similar ideologies, leading to cooperation between religious zealots and secular radicals; between ideologically- or theologically-driven terrorists and criminal entities (as has been the case in several terrorist attacks in Iraq, where criminal elements played critical roles in return for monetary compensation); between Sunni and Shi'a groups; and between individuals whose person-to-person contacts require no agreement between their respective headquarters.

A particularly interesting example is the Madrid Al Qaida cell, perhaps the most important cell broken up since 9/11. Muhammad Zouaydi, a key Al Qaida financier and the head of the cell, not only funded the Hamburg cell behind the 9/11 plot, but also dispatched a Madrid cell member to conduct pre-operational surveillance at the Twin Towers and other US landmarks a few years before the attacks. At the same time that he financed Al Qaida operations, Zouaydi also transferred money to the Hamas.

These relationships become all the more important to terrorists operating outside their home regions in their respective Diasporas. In the case of radical Islamist extremists, Diaspora communities in the West often serve as a radical melting pot, where like-minded individuals affiliated with different groups from geographically distinct regions assist one another for the sake of their larger cause. It is not uncommon to find a Tunisian member of an-Nada helping a Palestinian member of Hamas, or any number of other combinations of radical causes. Authorities therefore need to understand that terrorists do not carry membership cards in their wallets identifying themselves as members of a specific terrorist group, and that even if they did the phenomenon would not capture the full scope of the individual's terrorist affiliations.

The case of Abu Musab al Zarqawi (aka Fadel Nazzal Khalayleh) offers a particularly insightful perspective of the scope of the informal links, personal relationships and organizational crossovers between disparate terrorist operatives and groups. As the Zarqawi case makes abundantly clear, such networks of relationships are both geographically and organizationally diverse.

Zarqawi's links span the globe, including strong ties with terrorist groups in Turkey, Lebanon, Iraq, Iran, Jordan, Syria, Afghanistan, Germany, Britain, and elsewhere in Europe. The US Treasury highlighted his ties with Hizballah in its September 24, 2003 announcement, naming him and several of his associates as Specially Designated Global Terrorist (SDGT) entities.

Similar links between other Hizballah entities and international terrorist members and groups are equally illuminating regarding Hizballah's global reach. A case in point is Lebanese-born Bilal Khazal, now believed to be the senior Al Qaida operative in Australia, who is also suspected of ties with Hizballah and the al-Aqsa International Foundation. Both the CIA and British authorities have linked Khazal to Al Qaida, and the Australian government has deemed Khazal (currently residing in Sydney) a threat to national security and revoked his passport. While al-Aqsa primarily served as a Hamas front organization, Sheikh Moayad, the head of the al-Aqsa office in Yemen, was arrested in Germany and extradited to the United States for providing financial support to Al Qaida as well. Moayad proudly told an undercover FBI informant that he not only funded Hamas but also raised millions of dollars, recruited operatives, and supplied weapons to Al Qaida. According to one report, one of the foundation's offices in Europe also raised funds for the Hizballah.

Clearly, the assessment of a group's global presence entails not only the notation of the activities of its operational activists—those who pull the trigger, detonate the explosives or crash the airplane—but also the logistical and financial supporters that make such operations possible. If 9/11 taught us nothing else, we should all now recognize that logistical and financial support is critical to terrorist operations.

Hizballah has conducted terrorist operations in places as disparate as Thailand and Argentina. It operates logistical and financial support networks across the globe and maintains links to other international terror groups. By any standard, Hizballah represents a classic example of a terrorist group of global reach that should be a prioritized target in the war on terror.

Hizballah's Global Reach

Hizballah holds a particularly disturbing, though often overlooked, place in the matrix of international terror. Several studies have noted Hizballah's links with other groups, like the Treasury's announcement about Zarqawi, while others, such as a report compiled by the Council on Foreign Relations' Task Force on Terrorist Financing, highlight that "other Islamist terrorist organizations, Hamas and Hizballah specifically, often use the very same methods—and even the same institutions—[such as Al Qaida] to raise and move their money."

Published reports suggest that Al Qaida has formed additional tactical, ad-hoc alliances with a variety of terrorist organizations in order to cooperate on money laundering and other unlawful activities. And yet, the debate persists. Is Hizballah the "A-team of terrorists," as Deputy Secretary of State Richard Armitage suggests, or is Hizballah purely a "resistance" organization whose "role is limited to the Lebanese lands," as Syrian President Bashar al-Assad has insisted?

Following a careful assessment of Hizballah's global presence and operations, and based on research I conducted in the preparation of an upcoming book on the subject, I submit that Hizballah is indeed a terrorist group of global reach. Indeed, this conclusion is the consensus among the various intelligence professionals I have interviewed, including Israeli, Arab, American, Asian and European officials, and is also clear from the documentary evidence I have collected from sources as diverse as Filipino and Chilean law enforcement and intelligence agencies.

Moreover, Hizballah operatives—like those of other professional terrorist groups—melt into their environments and can be very difficult to identify. Consider a surveillance photo taken by Canadian intelligence officers, which captures a Hizballah member purchasing false identification for the procurement of dual-use technologies for Hizballah. Unlike Hizballah operatives patrolling the Lebanese-Israeli border, these members leave their yellow Hizballah bandanas and flags at home.

According to U.S. authorities, concern over the threat posed by Hizballah is well placed. FBI officials testified in February 2002 that "FBI investigations to date continue to indicate that many Hizballah subjects based in the United States have the capability to attempt terrorist attacks here should this be a desired objective of the group." Similarly, then-CIA Director George Tenet testified in February 2003 that "Hizballah, as an organization with capability and worldwide presence, is [Al Qaida's] equal, if not a far more capable organization."

Hizballah's Modus Operadi

Though Hizballah cells are not all identical, they do tend to display similar operational signatures in the form of typical *modi operandi*.

Subtle Infiltration: Hizballah operatives are expert at gaining entry to their target locations through extremely subtle infiltration. This should not come as a surprise, as many Hizballah operatives receive very sophisticated training both in Lebanon and in Iran from Iran's Ministry of Intelligence and Security (MOIS) and the Islamic Revolutionary Guard Corp (IRGC) al-Quds Brigades. Members of a Hizballah cell operating in Singapore in the late 1990s and into 2000 gained entry by exploiting a visa-waiver program similar to the one that was recently suspended in the United States. Once they arrived, they quickly married local women to legalize their presence. Members of a Hizballah cell in North Carolina, which raised significant sums of money for the group from the proceeds of an elaborate cigarette smuggling scam, accessed the US from South America using false documents, entered into sham marriages in Cyprus, and conducted their activities under multiple identities.

Fundraising: Hizballah cells are frequently involved in fundraising activities, even if they are primarily operational entities. Hizballah cells raise funds through charities acting as front organizations, as well as via criminal activities like cigarette smuggling, drug production and smuggling, and credit card or other types of fraud. Hizballah networks organize regular parlor meetings held in members' homes where a collection basket is passed around after watching Hizballah propaganda videos usually produced by al-Manar, the group's satellite television network. For example, the Charlotte network assembled regularly to watch videos of live Hizballah bombings in southern Lebanon prior to the Israeli withdrawal, then collected donations to support such activities. Hizballah operates front companies, and in South America the group is renowned for pirating multimedia and engaging in Mafia-style shakedowns of local Muslim businesses.

Recruiting Locals: Contrary to conventional wisdom, Hizballah is extremely adept at recruiting members from local populations in areas where they have networks on the ground. In Russia, Hizballah operatives recruited Sunni Palestinian students studying at Russian universities, while in Uganda they recruited Ugandan Shi'a students and sent them to study at an Iranian university where they also received military training together with Lebanese recruits in the use of small arms, bomb making, counter-interrogation techniques and escape planning. Before returning home, the Ugandans were provided with fictitious covers and instructed to establish an operational network in Uganda.

In Southeast Asia, the network that was behind the attempt to bomb the Israeli Embassy in Bangkok in 1994, as well as a series of other terrorist plots throughout the 1990s, was almost entirely Sunni. The leader of the network, Pandu Yudhawitna, was himself recruited by MOIS officers stationed in Malaysia in the early 1980s, and only later became the Southeast Asian point-man for Hizballah operations and support activities there.

After realizing that state troopers were frequently pulling their vans over for speeding on the way from North Carolina to Michigan, Charlotte cell members hired Caucasian women to drive their vans to elicit less suspicion.

Multi-functional: Hizballah cells are adept multi-taskers, responsible for a variety of logistical, financial and operational duties. They raise funds, recruit new members, conduct preoperational surveillance, provide logistical support, procure weapons and dual use technologies (for both Hizballah and Iran), and conduct operations.

Investigators in several countries have concluded independently that security services should avoid looking for cells that are strictly engaged in fundraising, logistical support or terrorist operations. Indeed, cells known only to have raised funds have later been found to have played active roles in terrorist operations, as was the case, for example, in the 1992 and 1994 suicide bombings in Argentina. In the words of one U.S. government official interviewed for this study, "Hizballah cells are always a bit operational."

Targeting US Interests—A Sampling

Indeed, Hizballah has conducted a wide variety of operations targeting not only Israeli and Jewish targets, but also the United States. Typically, academics opine that Hizballah has not targeted the United States since it bombed the US Embassy and marine barracks in the 1980's. In fact, there are several more recent instances of Hizballah activity targeting the US, consider the following sampling:

In 1989, Bassam Gharib Makki, a Hizballah operative and student in Germany, collected intelligence on Israeli, Jewish and American targets in Germany.

In 1989 and 1990, authorities apprehended a Hizballah cell operating in Valencia, Spain. The cell was caught smuggling weapons in a ship from Cyprus so that they could be pre-positioned and cached in Europe. After tracking that shipment, authorities found additional explosives that had already been stashed in Europe. It was determined that the cell had been targeting US and Israeli targets in Europe.

In 1997, Hizballah was found to be collecting intelligence on the US Embassy in Nicosia, Cyprus.

Throughout the mid- to late-1990s, Hizballah recruited Palestinian students studying in Russia, and collected intelligence on Israeli, Jewish and American targets there.

Throughout the 1990s, Hizballah members were active in Singapore, recruiting local Sunnis, collecting intelligence on Israeli and US ships in the Malacca Straits, and planning attacks. Authorities there uncovered a suicide speedboat attack very similar to the one that was thwarted about a year after 9/11 off Gibraltar.

Hizballah Terrorist Operations Abroad

Hizballah is well known for several international terrorist attacks, most notably the 1992 Israel; Embassy and 1994 AMIA suicide bombings in Argentina, and the 1995 Khobar Towers attack in Saudi Arabia. These, however, represent only two of Hizballah's foreign terrorist operations.

Europe as a launching pad: Hizballah has activated its members throughout Europe to assist operatives in exploiting Europe as a launching pad to enter Israel and conduct attacks or collect intelligence. In 1996, Hussein Makdad, a Lebanese citizen, entered Israel from Switzerland using a forged British passport. He was critically injured when a bomb he was assembling exploded in his Jerusalem hotel room. In 1997, a German convert to Islam, Stefan Smirnak, approached a Hizballah operative in Germany about committing a suicide attack in Israel. Several months later, Smirnak flew from Amsterdam to Tel Aviv with the intent of procuring an explosive to carry out a suicide bombing in Israel. Fawzi Ayoub, a Canadian of Lebanese descent, arrived in Israel on a boat travelling from Europe. Discarding his Canadian passport in Europe, he used a forged US passport, which he procured from a Hizballah operative he met in Europe, to enter Israel. He was subsequently arrested in Hebron, right around the time that Israeli authorities found a roadside explosive device in Hebron that had previously only been used by Hizballah in Lebanon. In 2001, Jihad Shuman, a British citizen of Lebanese descent, flew from Lebanon to Europe on his Lebanese passport, and then on to Israel using his British passport. Shuman stayed in Jerusalem, presumably on a mission of operational intelligence for a terrorist attack.

In some of these cases, the authorities have determined that the operatives entered Israel to conduct operations, while in other cases it remains unclear whether they entered Israel just to collect pre-operational surveillance, assist other operatives already there, or conduct attacks themselves. Significantly, each of these operatives is believed to have been trained by elements tied directly to Imad Mughniyeh, Hizballah's chief operations officer.

Operations in Southeast Asia: Hizballah operations in Southeast Asia throughout the 1990's are almost too many to count. Like the abovementioned infiltrations into Israel from Europe, Hizballah infiltrated at least one Malaysian operative into Israel to collect intelligence. After being recruited and undergoing Hizballah training, Zinal Bin-Talib entered Israel, collected intelligence, and returned home without the knowledge of Israeli authorities, who were only made aware of this penetration much later. Hizballah has conducted significant fundraising in Southeast Asia. It nearly succeeded in bombing the Israeli Embassy in Bangkok in 1994 and collected intelligence on synagogues in Manila and Singapore. Hizballah members procured and cached weapons in Thailand and the Philippines, checking on them periodically to ensure that the equipment was still operative in the event that they were called upon to conduct an attack at any given time. They collected intelligence pertaining to the El Al office in Bangkok, ships arriving in Singapore, and US Navy and Israeli merchant ships in the Malacca Straits. The Southeast Asian Hizballah network recruited many local Sunni Muslims, and sent several to Lebanon for training. They procured false and stolen passports, and recruited and trained local operatives to conduct potential attacks in Israel and in Australia.

Operations in Africa: Hizballah operatives in Africa help finance the group's activities by dealing in conflict diamonds in Sierra Leone and Liberia, a practice now used by Al Qaida, based on the model and contacts established by Hizballah. According to David Crane, the prosecutor for the Special Court in Sierra Leone, "Diamonds fuel the war on terrorism. Charles Taylor is harbouring terrorists from the Middle East, including Al Qaida and Hizballah, and has been for years." A telling example of the personality types involved in this activity is Ibrahim Bah. Bah is an affiliate of deposed Liberian strongman Charles Taylor, as well as a commander of the RUF rebels in Sierra Leone. Bah underwent military and terrorist training in Libya, Lebanon (where he fought with Hizballah units), and in Afghanistan. Over the course of his career, Bah also served as a personal bodyguard to Libya's Muamar Qadaffi and fought with Hizballah units in the Beka'a Valley in the 1980s.

Hizballah conducts extensive fundraising operations in Africa—as it does in other corners of the globe like South and North America—not only via illicit diamond trading but also through the local Shi'a expatriate community. In some cases, Shi'a donors are unwittingly conned into funding Hizballah, while in others they are knowing and willing participants in Hizballah's financing efforts.

As noted above, in one particularly interesting case in 2002, Ugandan officials disrupted a cell of Shi'a students who were recruited by Iranian intelligence agents and sent to study on scholarships at the Rizavi University in Mashhad, Iran. Upon their return, one student recruit named Shafri Ibrahim was caught, while another, Sharif Wadulu, is believed to have fled to one of the Gulf States. The two were trained by the MOIS, together with new Lebanese Hizballah recruits, and sent home with fictitious covers to establish an operational infrastructure.

Operations at other locations: Hizballah activity in South America has been well documented, including its frenetic activity in the Tri-border area. The group's activities received special attention in the wake of the 1992 bombing of the Israeli Embassy in Buenos Aires and the 1994 bombing of the AMIA Jewish community center there. The recently released Argentine indictment in the AMIA bombing reveals an extensive Hizballah operational presence in South America. A fact that is less known, however, is that Hizballah is also active in Chile, Venezuela, Cuba, Panama and Ecuador. Of particular concern to law enforcement officials throughout South America is Hizballah's increased activity in free trade zones, especially under the cover of import-export companies.

Intelligence officials are equally troubled by Hizballah activities in such diverse places as Romania, South Africa, Canada and Thailand.

Hizballah and Iranian Commanders

The most significant modus operandi characteristic of all Hizballah global operations—financial, logistical and operational—is that all Hizballah networks are overseen by, and in contact with, senior Hizballah and/or Iranian officials. In Charlotte North Carolina, Hizballah operatives reported directly to Sheikh Abas Haraki, a senior Hizballah military commander in South Beirut. Members of the Charlotte cell received receipts from Hizballah for their donations, including receipts from the office of the Hizballah spiritual leader at that time, Sheikh Mohammad Fadlallah.

The Charlotte cell was closely tied to a sister network in Canada that was primarily engaged in procuring dual-use technologies such as night vision goggles and laser range finders for Hizballah operational squads. The Canadian network was under the direct command of Hajj Hassan Hilu Lakis, Hizballah's chief military procurement officer.

In Southeast Asia, the Hizballah network operating there throughout the 1990's was under the command of a senior Mughniyah deputy named Abu Foul. As noted above, Iranian MOIS agents stationed in Malaysia originally recruited some of the Hizballah operatives there. Senior Hizballah operatives and Iranian agents were also involved in the 1995 Khobar Towers bombing in Saudi Arabia, in Hizballah efforts to smuggle weapons to Palestinian terrorists through Jordan, in Hizballah operations in South America—including the 1992 and 1994 Argentina bombings—and in the recruitment of students like those in Uganda. The key common thread running throughout these cases is the direct contact that each cell maintains with senior Hizballah and/or Iranian intelligence operatives.

Crossover Between Terrorism and "Resistance"

Many argue that the Hizballah is merely a "resistance" organization responding to Israeli occupation of disputed land. The distinction, which is apparently lost on most Western experts, is that the "resistance" groups in question perpetrate acts of terrorism such as suicide bombings to achieve their goals. But no goal, however legitimate, can justify the use of terrorist tactics and the killing of innocent civilians.

Moreover, even by Hizballah's own definition, the group's acts of terrorism and resistance are not purely compartmentalized. Indeed, the same Hizballah operatives are frequently involved in the group's terrorist activities and its support for Palestinian "resistance" (i.e. terrorist) groups like Hamas.

For example, Yousuf Aljouni and Abu al-Foul, two of the masterminds of the failed 1994 attempt to bomb the Israeli Embassy in Thailand, were subsequently apprehended in Jordan for smuggling weapons to Palestinian terrorists in 2001. In another case, Mohammad Dbouk, the one-time head of the Canadian procurement cell, underwent terrorist training in camps in Iran before serving Hizballah in Canada and, upon his return to Lebanon from Canada, provided preoperational surveillance for Hizballah attack squads working under the cover of Hizballah's satellite al-Manar television station. The preoperational footage that he filmed was used to plan Hizballah attacks on Israeli positions prior to the Israeli withdrawal from Lebanon, and the live footage of the actual attack was then used to produce propaganda videos of the type seized in the homes of the Charlotte cell members. Perhaps the most blatant example of this crossover between terrorism and resistance is the case of the Karin-A weapons smuggling ship. Though intended to supply 50 tons of military grade weapons to Palestinian terrorists, the operation was subcontracted to Hizballah by Iran and was overseen by Hajj Bassem, a senior Mughniyah deputy.

West Bank Foothold and International Plots

Recently, Hizballah has proactively mixed its "resistance" and terrorist activities by establishing a network of its own Palestinian cells in the West Bank. Hizballah's West Bank foothold not only threatens Israel with terrorist attacks there, but, in at least one case, a Palestinian Hizballah recruit sought to supplement his terror activities in Israel with attacks abroad.

Ghulam Mahmud Qawqa was arrested in 2003 for his role in al-Aqsa Martyrs Brigade bombings in Jerusalem. Subsequent investigation determined that he was also behind two international plots that were set in motion in late 2002. In one, he tasked a Lebanese woman living in Berlin to conduct surveillance on the Israeli Embassy there in an effort to target either the Embassy or the Israeli ambassador to Berlin, Shimon Stein. In a second operation, Qawqa asked a Jordanian friend living in China to facilitate his travel arrangements to that destination, and at the same time sought the assistance of a Hizballah operative in planning the assassination of the Israeli ambassador to China, Yitzhak Shelef.

Avoiding Past Mistakes

Hizballah maintains ad-hoc, person-to-person contacts with Al Qaida terrorists, but this is not the main reason for prioritizing the group as a target in the war on terror. Its own activities are far more significant. As is clear from all of the above cases, and many others, Hizballah is indeed a terrorist group of global reach. Current intelligence assessments from a variety of security services concur that Hizballah remains capable and intent on attacking Israeli, American and other Western targets and therefore poses a current, serious threat. Hizballah chief Sheikh Hassan Nasrallah, as well as many other Hizballah officials, makes this perfectly clear in his bellicose, threatening statements. In the wake of the Iraq war, these threats have become even more pronounced, venomous and unqualified.

Past experience teaches us that failure to deal with the real and immediate threat posed by Hizballah today will have severe and painful repercussions tomorrow. It took the international community more than a decade to get up to speed on the threat posed by Al Qaida. During that time, Al Qaida successfully built an entrenched and sophisticated international logistical and financial support network of the kind that eventually facilitated the attacks of September 11th. There is no question that Hizballah is engaged in exactly the same infrastructure-building today. Given our experience in September 2001, it should be abundantly clear that we ignore such activity, and the acute security threat it represents, at our peril.

The Profile of the Modern Terrorist

Prof. Ariel Merari

Tel-Aviv University, Israel.

I find it very appropriate that this symposium is dedicated to the memory of the late Ehud Sprinzak, one of the most important researchers of terrorism, a very unique researcher and scientist. I knew Ehud for more than 20 years, and I have always admired his work. Among other qualities that he had, such as a great sense of humor and a very direct approach to people, he was also very special in his emphasis of the need to maintain contact with terrorists, and talk to them, in order to understand them. Many people around the world study terrorism without bothering to ever talk to terrorists. Many of those researchers on terrorism have never seen a terrorist with their own eyes. Ehud spent many hours talking to extremists, including actual terrorists, and on many occasions, in conferences and private conversations, I heard him urging people to try to obtain first-hand information on terrorism. First-hand information comes primarily from interviewing people, from listening to them. I think this was one of his great, long-lasting contributions to the culture of the study of terrorism.

In a way, my talk here is connected to this theme that Ehud advocated, because discussing the profile of a terrorist is meaningless unless you possess some factual information, some empirical knowledge. Empirical psychological knowledge can only be gained by interviewing the involved parties.

Admittedly, studying the psychology of terrorists is not easy. The difficulties stem from the fact that terrorist organizations are clandestine, and terrorists do not willingly make themselves available for interviewing, certainly not for filling out psychological questionnaires and tests. They are even less willing to participate in psychological laboratory experiments. This can occasionally be done, under some circumstances, but it is not easy. Three years ago or so, I even organized a conference with terrorists in Paris. There was no other country in the West that would so willingly host a conference with terrorists, which was a great advantage. The participants at that conference—about 25 in number—were a mixture of academics and terrorists. In addition to presentations and discussions, we even ran a simulation in which mixed groups of terrorists and academics played terrorists or government authorities. This was an interesting experience, which demonstrates that a direct examination of terrorists, albeit not easy, is possible under some circumstances. Still, there is a dire lack of empirical data on the profile of terrorists, especially regarding the psychological (rather than demographic) qualities involved. Nevertheless, this question needs to be addressed here, and efforts must be made to provide as accurate a response as possible, based on existing knowledge.

Before querying whether there *is* a new terrorist profile, we must first ask whether there was an old profile. I am sorry to say that, by and large, the answer is no, with the exception of minimal obvious observations, such as that terrorists tend to be young and unmarried. Despite the scarcity of reliable empirical studies, the consensus among serious researchers who have studied empirical data is that there is no universal terrorist profile, meaning that there is no "terrorist type" to speak of. This is hardly unexpected. I would be surprised if the case were otherwise, because terrorists come from a range of diverse cultures; they act in very dissimilar political contexts, and the meaning of being a terrorist differs in various countries and settings.

In addition to these aspects, I think that the term "terrorist" is too general. What is a terrorist? A terrorist is the group leader or the ideologue; a terrorist is one of a whole bunch of individuals that fill a variety of logistical roles in the organization—the moneyman, the forger; and of course, a terrorist is the man who can assassinate a person point-blank, or detonate himself in a suicide attack. All of these individuals are terrorists. Can we really expect all of these persons to share personality traits that make them distinguishable from the general population? This is not very likely. Indeed, without going into the details of the few reliable studies based on empirical evidence, the consensus is that there is no universal terrorist personality.

Even when endeavoring to be much more specific, the study of a very particular type of terrorist will not yield common traits. In this country, studies were conducted years ago in which Palestinian hostage-takers were interviewed and given a variety of psychological tests. These terrorists shared the same culture, the same nationality, and the same type of mission, but nonetheless they still had very few common characteristics: Most of them displayed a high level of aggressiveness in personality tests, which may be regarded either as a personality trait or as a response to their imprisonment, or both; about half of them had a criminal record; and about half came from broken homes. But there was no common psychopathology and no shared personality type. By and large, their aggressiveness and the other characteristics were probably a result of a process of selection. Their aggressiveness and recklessness were the criteria according to which they were selected from among other terrorists to participate in these missions. But this was not the profile of the average member of the groups that sent them, such as the DFLP or Fatah at that time. To summarize this aspect, and judging by past experience, the likelihood of finding a terrorist profile is not very great.

Is there a "new terrorist profile?" What does the concept of a "new terrorist" mean? In what way do new terrorists differ from old ones? For quite a few years Bruce Hoffman has promoted the notion that terrorism has become progressively lethal, increasingly deadly, and less and less discriminate.[69] Today's terrorists are more deadly, more willing to kill people in great numbers, and less discriminate in their targeting than past terrorists. Does this imply that they have different personality types than bygone terrorists? Here again the answer is disappointing, if you are a psychologist who is looking for "the" terrorist type, "the" epitome of the terrorist personality. There are a number of empirical studies based on various methods that suggest that today's terrorists, such as Al Qaida members or Palestinian terrorists, are not all cut out of the same cloth, and there are no clear identifying marks that distinguish them from the other members of the community from which they come. There is a very good summary of Al Qaida members' profiles done by Marc Sageman.[70] He found that these are just ordinary people. Most of

---

69 For example see Bruce Hoffman, *Inside Terrorism*, London: Victor Golancz, 1998.

70 Marc Sageman, Statement to the National Commission on Terrorist Attacks Upon the United States, July 9, 2003. Available at: www.9/11commission.gov/hearings/ hearing3/

them come from middle-class families and are educated—one third of them have a full university education. Two thirds were devout Muslims, but one third were not. The latter drank alcohol, smoked, frequented nightclubs and dated women. Some of them were not even fanatically religious. And, most important, they displayed no psychological pathology to speak of. By and large, they were ordinary people that, by Sageman's account, drifted into the organization. They drifted into the organization as a form of social activity, or as a way to avoid alienation; this is especially true of those living in Western countries, who found a welcoming hub in the group. They were taken into the bosom of the loving organization, where they discovered friendship and a cause. But these were ordinary people.

Another study was conducted by Jerry Post and Ehud Sprinzak, who interviewed Palestinian terrorists incarcerated in Israeli prisons. Their findings were similar.[71] The terrorists whom they interviewed were common people, with no discernible psychopathology, and the main motivating force for joining the group was its social value. To quote just one sentence from their article, one of the interviewed terrorists said, "My social status was greatly enhanced by joining the organization, by joining terrorist activity. I got a lot of respect from my acquaintances and from the young people in the village."

Another novelty in terrorism is the phenomenon of suicide attacks. Should we attribute this form of terrorism to the emergence of a new type of terrorist? Studies conducted on suicide terrorists by myself and others have used, inter alia, the method of psychological autopsy. As it is impossible to interview and test dead persons, the psychological study of suicide uses the method of psychological autopsy as a substitute for direct interviews and tests. This method relies on interviews with families and friends, and the gathering of other data for reconstructing the suicide's personality, as well

---

witness_sageman.htm. Accessed: Aug. 18, 2003; also: Marc Sageman, Escape from Alienation: Drifting into Al Qaida. Lecture at the American Psychological Association's Annual Convention, Chicago, August, 2002.

71 J. Post, E. Sprinzak, & L. Denny, "The terrorists in their own words: Interviews with 35 incarcerated Middle Eastern terrorists." Terrorism and Political Violence, 2003, 15 (1), pp. 171-184.

as the motivations and circumstances that led him or her to commit suicide. Interviews with the families of most of the Palestinian suicide terrorists prior to the current Intifada clearly indicated that these were ordinary people. This impression was reinforced in interviews with some living terrorists, would-be suicides who survived because the explosive charge that they carried had malfunctioned or because they were apprehended en route to the target. Some trainers and people who prepared the suicide candidates and dispatched them on their mission were also interviewed. The findings of this study contradicted some popular beliefs vis-à-vis terrorist suicides. Clearly, the actual and potential suicides were not insane, nor did they share a common personality pattern. They were not particularly poor; in socioeconomic terms, they represented a fair cross-section of the Palestinian population. Their level of education was higher than the Palestinian average. Most of them were not exceptionally religious, nor was religion their key motivation. As they stated it, their motivation was primarily nationalist. Religious sentiments were an ancillary factor in many cases, but not the main driving force. The fact that religion was not the principal motivation should not surprise us. Contrary to common belief, most of the suicide terrorists in Lebanon were affiliated with secular groups. In Sri Lanka, the Tamil Tigers, who have carried out about 170 suicide attacks, are not motivated by religious fanaticism, but by ethnic-separatist aspirations. The Kurdish Labor Party (PKK), a group that has carried out 15 suicide attacks, is a Marxist organization. Clearly, therefore, religion is not a necessary characteristic of suicide terrorists and it probably is not a sufficient factor either.

In the great majority of the cases, the willingness to carry out a suicide attack could not be explained by personal trauma attributed to the enemy or as a matter of personal revenge. Only in a few cases, had the suicide lost a close family member and only in a minority of the cases had the suicide served time in jail or been wounded or beaten in clashes with the Israeli security forces. In fact, the surviving would-be-suicides explained their readiness to carry out suicide attacks as the consequence of national, rather than personal, humiliation.

All in all, the most salient feature of the suicides was their ordinariness. In fact, most of them were fairly marginal people in their community. To use Hannah Arendt's phrase, in this respect the terrorist suicides represent the banality of evil. How, then, can we explain their becoming suicide terrorists? The answer involves two main factors. The first is the prevalent public atmosphere. Currently, in the Palestinian community, becoming a shahid by carrying out a suicide attack is considered the ultimate form of patriotism and heroism. Posters of shahids are on every wall. The media exalt them. Cassettes with songs in their honor are sold everywhere. Their families are respected. Children play a popular game: "I am a Shahid." In this atmosphere, many youngsters, without comprehending the full meaning of the act, say "I also want to become a shahid." They volunteer for a suicide mission or acquiesce when approached by an organization's operative with the suggestion to carry out a suicide attack (the partial data available suggest that about half of the suicides volunteer on their own initiative, and the other half are first approached by an organization's recruiter).

But volunteering fired by a surge of zeal to die is no guarantee that the young enthusiast will live up to his promise weeks later. He may still change his mind a hundred times, especially as the moment of implementation draws nearer and what initially was an abstract possibility of glorious death becomes a close certainty of ceasing to live. And here is the second major element in the making of the "shahid:" This is a group process that builds up and maintains the commitment in a way that insures that the candidate cannot jump off the boat without losing all self-respect, and certainly the respect of his peers in the community. Having given his initial consent, the candidate is actually entrapped in the process. To be sure, some of the recruits apparently do continue all the way with full conviction, until the moment of explosion. Some, however, hesitate or even regret their rash volunteering, but the psychological price of breaking their commitment is very high. This irrevocable commitment is cemented through continuous indoctrination and, most important, via a formal ritual in which the candidate declares his commitment to carry out a suicide attack in front of a television camera. In this recorded statement, the candidate almost invariably refers to himself as "the living martyr" (al-shahid al-hai). Not only is it very difficult to break such a formal commitment, but in the wake of this statement, the candidate's mood is resigned, and he accepts death as inevitable.

To sum up, perhaps the most salient feature of the "new terrorism" is that suicide attacks are not the product of a different personality type of the alleged "new terrorists." Various types of persons may, and do, end up suicide terrorists. The process involves the terrorist organization's decision to adopt this tactic, a community atmosphere that generates volunteers, and group processes that nail down and sustain the volunteers' commitment. The notion that suicide terrorism is a group, rather than an individual, phenomenon is underscored by the fact that not a single case has been recorded of a suicide terrorist who carried out his/her act of suicide on a personal whim. There is no individual Palestinian who simply decided, "I am going to kill myself and some Jews," or a Tamil who said, "I shall kill myself and a government official," got himself a hand grenade or an explosive charge, and carried out his decision on his own. In all of the cases, with no exception, it was an organization that arranged the attack, recruited the suicide, determined the time and the target, arranged the explosive charge, and saw to it that the suicide was escorted to the target, to make sure that he really went through with it. Contrary to the title of my presentation, therefore, the key does not lie in the profile of the terrorist but rather in the profile of the group.

Finally, I wish to offer a few words concerning the implications of these findings. The assertion that the true crucial factors are not the personality of the terrorist in general, and the suicide terrorist in particular, but rather public atmosphere and the terrorist group's influence, has important ramifications concerning counter-measures. First, it is vital to recognize that the most important tactic against suicide attacks is to confront the attitude of the population that breeds them. When the population in question comes to perceive suicide attacks as unjustified, immoral or damaging to its own interests, there will be far fewer volunteers for such missions. It should, however, be understood that changing public attitudes cannot be achieved by mere propaganda; this progress must involve real political steps.

A second conclusion is related to measures directed against the terrorist group. A person who is determined to die may not be easily deterred. But as explained above, suicide attacks are a group, rather than an individual, venture, and a group can almost always be deterred. The only exception to the rule is some cults that believe that doomsday is imminent and seek death in order to resurrect later. But even ideologically extreme groups such as Hamas, for instance, can be deterred. Practically no terrorist group aspires to destroy itself with the enemy. The group is willing to sacrifice members but wants to continue to exist as an organization, and that is where our efforts should be directed.

Terrorism Forecasting & Technology

Terrorism Assessment, Forecasting and Preemptive Response Model

Dr. Joshua Sinai

Anser (On detail to the U.S. Government—all views expressed in this article are the author's own).

In order to assess the type or spectrum of warfare that a terrorist group is likely to use in its operations, this paper attempts to develop a new "indications and warning" (I&W) methodology. The resulting tool kit will comprehensively and systematically map all relevant and significant indicators, sub-indicators and observables that need to be considered in forecasting a group's likely terrorist warfare.

A key proposition is that most of the current threat assessments fail to adequately assess the likelihood and magnitude of the types of threats posed by contemporary terrorism. This is due to three fundamental problems in their approaches. First, many threat assessments focus exclusively on two types of warfare—"conventional" and "non-conventional" (CBRN)—but leave out the gradations of warfare that are more prevalent in terms of their actual or potential impact. In this more comprehensive approach, such gradations of warfare would include conventional low impact (CLI), conventional high impact (CHI), and low or high impact CBRN.[72]

Second, most of the current approaches do not adequately correlate the factors that generate the types of warfare that terrorist groups are likely to resort to in order to achieve their objectives, particularly in terms of the nature of their leadership, motivation, and strategy. Other factors also not taken into account include accelerators, triggers, and the numerous constraints involved in the transition by terrorist groups from CLI to CHI and to CBRN warfare. Above all, most of the current approaches fail to address the crucial factor of the spectrum of disincentives and constraints that are likely to deter most

---

72 In this approach, CLI refers to 'low impact' attacks involving relatively 'few' casualties or physical damage, such as detonating explosives or shootings; CHI refers to the use of conventional means to inflict massive casualties, such as 9/11 type attacks; while CBRN refers to the use of chemical, biological, radiological, nuclear weapons and devices.

terrorist groups away from CBRN warfare, particularly when they can resort to conventional explosives which have become more lethal and "catastrophic" in their impact. As a result, most of the current approaches tend to lump all terrorist groups currently operating on the international scene as potential CBRN actors, without an adequate understanding of which terrorist groups are likely or unlikely to transition not only from CLI to CHI, but from CHI to CBRN warfare.

In this approach, a trichotomous outcome (CLI, CHI, or CBRN warfare) is hypothesized to predict the types of warfare most likely to be engaged in by terrorist groups. The pre-incident activities by terrorist groups are the independent variables (X), while the trichotomous outcome is the dependent variable (Y). As discussed later on, the independent variables are related to each other, so they need to be correlated in combination. The premise is that if one can collect this type of intelligence information about terrorist groups it will be possible to attain a sufficient predictive accuracy, while recognizing that there will always remain a certain percent of "real world" uncertainty built into any I&W forecasting system.

The Pre-Incident Four Phases of Terrorism's 31 I&W Indicator Categories

Group Formation ➲	Plan ➲	Develop ➲	Execute
Societal Conditions	Decisive Meeting	Acquisition	Tactics
Radical Subcultures	Recruitment	Development/ Production	Security
Types of groups	Training	Testing	Communication
Leadership		Weaponization	Logistics
Motivation		Storage Facilities	Surveillance
Strategy			Targeting
Organization			Internal Hurdles
Funding			External Hurdles

Group Formation ⊃	Plan ⊃	Develop ⊃	Execute
Front Organizations (Commercial)			
Constituency			
Foreign Group Linkages			
State Sponsor			
Accelerators ⬈			
Triggers ⬈			

⬈ **Indicates transition to next phase.**

The following diagram displays the ordered grouping of the I&W indicators by phases along the lethality and propensity axes (the phased ordering of the indicators is for analytic purposes only):

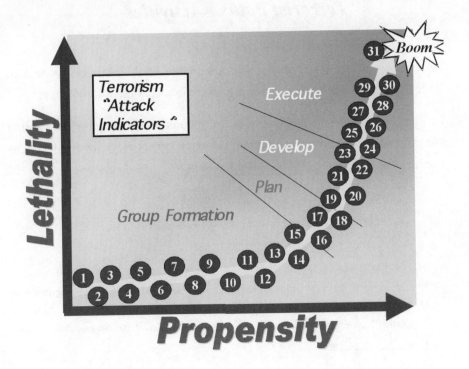

The following diagram displays the role of indications and warning during the pre-incident's terrorist activities/governmental intelligence response process.[73]

Responding to Pre-incident Paths / Activities

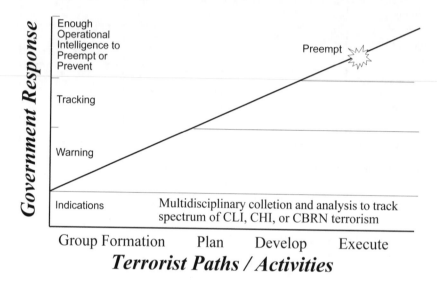

Terrorist Paths / Activities

Developing an accurate, timely, and actionable I&W indicators system to forecast a terrorist group's warfare proclivity involves the following steps÷

First, a threat assessment needs to be formulated that will generate warning "flags" that indicate a terrorist group's "attack potential." Several formulas can be used to derive a group's "attack potential."

---

73 This diagram is based, with modifications, on "Report of the Competency Panel on Operational Intelligence," in DOD Responses To Transnational Threats: Volume III, Supporting Reports (Washington, DC: Defense Science Board 1997 Summer Study Task Force, February 1998), p. 5.

- **Intention + Capability = Threat**

- **Threat + Indicators (activities/observables) = Warning**

- **Warning + Adversary Vulnerability = Risk Assessment**

- **Intention + Capability + Accelerators/Triggers + Overcoming Hurdles + Adversary Vulnerability = Attack Indicators/Attack Potential**

Second, a terrorist group's attack potential is derived from formulating hypotheses, which are broad explanatory statements that generate factors, which are more specific indicators suggesting a type of terrorist warfare proclivity. Indicators need to be considered in combination because no single factor is likely to indicate a particular warfare proclivity. Indicators can be combined to generate a group's warfare proclivity by performing four tasks:

- Task 1: *Identify the key observable CLI/CHI/CBRN* characteristics concerning the 31 I&W indicator categories (i.e., information available to analysts from various sources) regarding terrorist group motivations, capabilities and access to weapons, devices and delivery systems, as well as accelerators, triggers, and internal and external hurdles, that would indicate a proclivity or disinclination to engage in "catastrophic" warfare.

- Task 2: Determine *how to properly* weight those indicators/observables in order to assign lower or higher weights to those characteristics associated with potential CLI/CHI/CBRN proclivities that indicate a group is likely to embark on a particular type of warfare. For example, the indicators might be weighted by a rating system on a scale of 1 to 10, with 1 being the lowest and 10 being the highest threat potential, indicating the presence of the necessary motivation and operational capability by a terrorist group to carry out a particular type of attack.

- Task 3: Provide a quantifiable system for aggregating the weights assigned to the observable characteristics in order to arrive at an overall CLI/CHI/CBRN threat scoring that accurately indicates the likelihood that a group is planning an attack exhibiting the characteristics of a particular type of warfare.

- Task 4: Set an appropriate numerical threshold for those aggregated weights to indicate a probability that a group will resort to CLI or CHI or CBRN warfare, thus reaching a point to issue an appropriate warning concerning that group. The warning may be take the form of distinct colors to indicate the spectrum of warfare, such as green, yellow or red warnings.

However, unlike an I&W system for "conventional" terrorism that must effectively warn about a "conventional" type attack (for which there would also be a much higher probability, although lower casualties), a CLI/CHI/CBRN-oriented I&W system must be customized to focus on the likelihood that a particular terrorist group has attained either of the three types of warfare operational capability and that it intends to carry out a CLI/CHI/or CBRN type attack for which there would be a spectrum of probabilities ranging from low to high, including lower to higher consequences in terms of casualties and panic throughout society caused by one of the three types of attack.

Moreover, there are significant differences between "conventional" and CBRN warfare in terms of their types of weapons, devices and delivery systems, all of which will affect the way an I&W system will be designed. For example, the lead-time needed by a terrorist group to develop the capability to launch a nuclear attack is much greater than the time needed to prepare a biological, chemical, radiological or conventional attack. Therefore, the I&W indicators for the former will probably be based on a much more comprehensive list of factors, developed over a longer period of time, than for the latter's weapons, devices and delivery systems. Similarly, the threshold for warning about a possible nuclear terrorist attack is probably lower than that for a biological, chemical, radiological (BCR), or "conventional" attack, because the consequences of the former (and, therefore, the probable reactions of law enforcement agencies and military forces) are likely to be much more severe than for most terrorist attacks.

Thus, the I&W system for CLI/CHI/or CBRN warfare should be based on a series of databases and attributes for each of the CLI/CHI/or CBRN weapons and devices that the terrorist group under examination may be considering. As a result, one database of I&W attributes could examine the characteristics regarding motivations and operational capabilities by the terrorist group to determine which kinds of CLI/CHI/or CBRN weapons, devices and delivery systems they are most likely to employ. The second database of I&W attributes would identify the key characteristics that an analyst should look for in determining whether a group is becoming more or less likely to actually launch an attack for which they have the theoretical capability.

The objective of developing such an I&W methodology is to provide the analytical community with a tool kit to chart as many significant indicators (including sub-indicators and observables) as possible against which to collect information and data. Once correlated¬ the data would provide the necessary aggregation to issue warnings at the earliest possible timeframe that a group is likely to employ a "worrisome" type of warfare.

Such an objective, however, is inherently limited in several respects. First, without penetrating a group with one's own operatives or debriefing defectors, it is difficult to obtain tactical intelligence about a terrorist group's intentions, capabilities, and targeting. Thus, without such optimal counterintelligence conditions, any predictive analytic tool can only raise a warning flag based on secondary, not "primary," indicators about a certain terrorist group to generate a spectrum of potential "worrisome" scenarios, as opposed to pinpointing the timeframe for an actual attack.

Second, some of the new terrorist groups are loosely affiliated, ad hoc groupings that coalesce for a single operation, leaving few 'footprints' or 'signatures' of their activity, thus making it difficult for an analyst to monitor their activities and intentions.[74]

Third, additional limitations include (1) the difficulty of monitoring CLI/CHI/ or CBRN-associated activities by groups that engage in clandestine activities;

---

74 Stephen R. Bowers and Kimberly R. Keys, "Technology and Terrorism: The New Threat for the Millenium," Conflict Studies, No. 309, May 1998, p. 18.

(2) the need for significant lead time in tracking high-technology based terrorist attacks; and (3) even once information is gathered about a group's activities, there is the problem of aggregating all the indicators, because the likelihood of a group turning to CLI/CHI/or CBRN terrorism will probably be more a function of the interaction of several indicators than the force of any single indicator alone.

Nevertheless, despite these inherent shortcoming, an effective I&W methodology can provide analysts and counter-terrorism planners with a conceptual approach "to collate diverse sources of information and to understand complex relationships and data."[75]

To display the pre-incident's processes, paths and links involved in the likelihood that a terrorist group will resort to CLI/CHI/or CBRN warfare, this analysis groups the I&W indicators into four phases. These four phases are distinguished for analytical purposes and, in reality, some of the indicators or phases could be carried out contemporaneously or bypassed altogether. Moreover, within these four phases, the I&W indicators should be considered in combination because no single factor has sufficient independent explanatory value.

Phase I – the Group Formation phase

Phase II – the Planning phase

Phase III – the Developmental phase

Phase IV – the Execution phase

These four phases of the pre-incident process can be further broken down into ten levels of analysis:

- First, which geographic areas/states require monitoring for precipitating societal conditions (#1) and the proliferation of radical subcultures (#2) that might give rise to terrorist group formations?

---

75 Ibid., p. 19.

- Second, which particular terrorist groups (#3) are inclined, in terms of their leadership (#4), motivation (#5) and strategy (#6), to transition from conventional to CBRN warfare, and why would they choose CBRN "catastrophic" type warfare when "conventional" warfare might be sufficiently lethal?

- Third, what is the nature of the terrorist group's core constituency (#11) and how would it react to mass casualty/CBRN-type attacks as opposed to "low casualty" attacks with conventional weapons (although certain CBRN weapons might result in few casualties but mass panic throughout society)?

- Fourth, what kinds of accelerators (#14) and triggers (#15) are likely to drive terrorist leaders to plan a "high casualty" as opposed to a "low casualty" type attack, including attack dates?

- Fifth, what kinds of organizational (#7), funding (#8), recruitment (#17), acquisition (#19), development (#20), and logistical (#27) capabilities will a terrorist group need to attain the operational capability to execute either a "conventional" or CBRN attack?

- Sixth, in terms of the terrorist group's targeting options, what vulnerable 'key targeting (#29) points' are they most interested in attacking and are there certain key anniversaries around which they are likely to attack?

- Seventh, how does a terrorist group's decision to attack a particular target affect their choice of CBRN weapons, devices and delivery systems?

- Eighth, can the terrorist group embark on terrorist warfare on its own or with the support of a state sponsor (#3)?

- Ninth, what internal (#30) and external (#31) hurdles must terrorist groups overcome in order to execute a CBRN attack?

- Finally, what can the targeted adversary do during the pre-incident process to harden its defenses or pre-emptively respond against the spectrum of potential terrorist attacks?

Applying these 31 indicator categories to currently operating or emerging terrorist groups will reveal whether a group is planning an attack, its motivation and strategy, the type (or types) of weapons it plans to use (particularly "conventional" or CBRN), and its likely targeting. In such a way, this methodology enables an analyst to correlate along the pre-incident's four phases a terrorist group's internal factors (such as the nature of its leadership, motivation and strategy, organization, funding, recruitment, training, front organizations, constituency, logistical network, and surveillance of potential targets), with external factors (such as linkages with foreign groups, state sponsors, and foreign suppliers), as well as potential accelerators and triggers (such as access on the grey or black markets to needed components or devices, or a dramatic event that would precipitate a group to take drastic action), and a group's capability to overcome various internal and external hurdles (such as defections, breakdowns in security, testing failures or accidents with devices, or monitoring or penetration of a group by external intelligence or counter-terrorism organizations), in order to ascertain a group's "attack potential." Thus, if these indicator categories and their sub-indicators and observables could be correlated—recognizing that some indicators are more significant and have higher quantifiable weighting properties than others—such analysis might indicate increasing threat possibilities, including the possible resort to conventional or single or multiple CBRN weapons and devices, and their likely targeting.

Once the methodology yields the appropriate I&W information concerning terrorist groups warfare proclivity, then an analyst can utilize a tiered approach to develop a spectrum of warnings. Filter sets can be used to focus attention on current or emerging terrorist groups most likely to embark on CLI/CHI/or CBRN type warfare. A tiered approach can be used to identify groups likely to embark on CLI/CHI/or CBRN warfare, with increasingly "tight" filters for moving a group from CLI to CHI and the higher tier CBRN warfare.

Tier 1 (CBRN/CHI)	Alert	1-3?
Tier 2 (CHI)	Suspect	4-7?
Tier 3	Possible	8-10?
Tier 4	Potential	11-15?

Once sufficient "attack indicator" information and data coalesce to issue warnings about a group's imminent warfare proclivity, then other agencies or personnel would be tasked operationally to pre-empt or prevent a terrorist group from carrying out an attack, if such a governmental pre-emptive capability exists.

In such a way, a robust I&W methodology can be made sufficiently comprehensive and systematic to exploit all possible relevant indicators involved in the pre-incident process, and yet not be too general or abstract to be of practical use.

CBRN terrorist warfare is likely to pose a significant threat in the 21st century as a result of the confluence of motivation—particularly in terms of less constraints—technical capabilities (especially in assembling crude devices), wider availability of CBRN materiel (such as from the republics of the former Soviet Union), and involvement by state sponsors (such as Iran or North Korea). This analysis is intended to highlight some of the internal and external factors, requirements and hurdles that need to be considered in assessing a terrorist group's current and future development status and operational capability to conduct CBRN warfare. Correlating these internal and external factors and hurdles would make it possible to assess which terrorist groups and state sponsors are likely to embark on CBRN warfare, the types of adaptations and changes they would require to transition to such warfare, the types of weapons and targeting they are likely to pursue (including the possible resort to single or multiple CBRN weapons and devices), the timelines for such attacks, and vulnerabilities that could be exploited by foreign intelligence and counter-terrorism agencies to constrain terrorist groups--and, when applicable, state sponsors--from embarking on such warfare.

Hopefully, such a conceptual approach will make it possible for the counter-terrorism community, whether policy makers, law enforcement or military operators, or analysts to efficiently calibrate their resources to intervene at the earliest possible phases to influence, pre-empt, deter, and prevent terrorist actions, whether CLI, CHI, or CBRN.

The Evolution of Terrorism:
The Technological Factor

Michael Hopmeier

*Chief, Unconventional Concepts,
Inc., USA*

Gilead Shenhar

*Advisor, Disaster Response and
Emergency Preparedness, USA*

One of the key issues I think that we need to address in the future is the impact of technology as it becomes more widely available—on terrorists, on society, and on our ability to combat terrorism.

I'm sure we've all heard of some of the more recent attacks or attempts that have occurred, such as the use of surface-to-air missiles against an El-Al aircraft.

We're aware of the wide-based use of e-mail, of encryption technology, and the general availability of communications—to terrorists and to communities and people throughout the world. This is perhaps one of the most significant impacts on the ability to engage in crime or terrorism. By the same token, society itself, by its dependence on technology is becoming more vulnerable.

In Milwaukee, a major city in the United States, there was a relatively minor outbreak of an enteric stomach disease. It caused widespread impact throughout the city, yet it was a result of a relatively minor breakdown within the water purification system.

Society is very dependent on integrated technology. On Friday, August 13th, 2003, we had large power outages throughout the United States—all from what appears to be a single natural incident or occurrence.

However, technology is also of benefit to those who have to fight terrorism. For example, we hope to make use of technology for early detection of biological material and agents. Another technology that we are looking at uses various sensors to identify particular and unique signatures associated with explosives.

Perhaps at the heart of what we're all trying to do is address what *is* terrorism and how to counter it. Twenty-three hundred years ago, Sun Tzu Wu said,

"Kill one, terrify a thousand." That is probably the heart of what we're trying to deal with. The goal of the terrorist in general is to affect society in some way. In order to affect society, the people within the society have to know what is going on.

There are three key aspects that I think we need to look at in addressing technology in the context of terrorism: One, technology certainly helps the terrorist, whether we look at the wide availability of communications, such as e-mail and cellular phones, encryption technology, or other technologies such as timers, electronics, cheap sensors. All of those are used—and have been used—in many ways and in many different incidents by the terrorist. In fact, the use of technology is only limited by the terrorist's innovation. Secondly, in many ways, technology hurts society as well. It makes society more vulnerable. As noted in the power blackout that we had, one relatively minor incident removed electricity and power from roughly one third of the United States. You may recall just a few years ago the rolling blackouts in the state of California. Again, this indicated the reliance of our society has on inter-connected technologies. Finally, and perhaps most importantly, technology also helps society, specifically in trying to combat terrorism. It adds to our communities, to our different professionals, to the ability to exchange information, to the ability to detect terrorists, potentially model their goals and their intent and stop them before they can act.

Some of the generalized results of technology: As noted, it has made terrorists more effective. Explosives and weapon technologies are generally available today, as are communications, information, and coordination. And perhaps the most important tool of the terrorist, unintentional though it is, is the media—the rapid and effective ability to spread information throughout the entire world. Unquestionably, the media is vital to society, yet it can be used in many different ways. As a tool of the terrorist, it is very effective in making society aware of attacks and the intent of the terrorist. Secondly, as noted, technology has generally made society more vulnerable to terrorism. Not only through the use of the media to make information more well known, but also by providing tools directly to the terrorist. Sensor technologies, explosives, and weapons technology are all part of the toolbox that the terrorist can use. However, better coordination among agencies, improved intelligence, modeling and simulation, the ability to remotely detect terrorists, application of technologies—such as remotely sensing intentions or determining patterns of many people widely spaced throughout the world—are all capabilities based on technology which help us—the anti-terrorists if you will—try and perform our jobs.

When we look at the evolution of terror, we can look at it as the sum of capabilities and motivation. Capabilities are the combination of the weapons and vulnerabilities and this is where technology has the greatest influence. But we also have to consider the motivation: such issues as religion, social issues, nationalism, and a wide array of others.

Today's modern terrorist builds on a number of different capabilities: innovation, courage in their own mind, simplicity (trying to make systems as simple as possible and attacks as non-complex as they can be made), and finally, motivation. The technology here is important, but it is not nearly as important as the individual, the terrorist, his goals and his intent, and his ability to carry out his mission.

But we also have to consider that technology is not a simple addition of individual tools. It is greater than the sum. Simple devices—things like hand-held communicators, notebook computers, cellular phones and flight simulation games—all of these contributed, in one way or another, to the attacks of September 11th. What is important to recognize is that it is not a question of any one, two, or a group of individual technologies, but it is the sum of all of those technologies taken together in combination with the intelligence, motivation, and creativity of the terrorist.

In looking at how the sophistication of attacks rather than the sophistication of technologies has developed, we see that the early attacks were relatively simple attacks, such as assassination. As time went on, we reached the ultimate in sophistication, that of the true smart weapon: the suicide bomber.

The availability of technology is increasing; new tools and new capabilities are developed every day. Cell phones worldwide are becoming ubiquitous. Use of computers is everywhere. Even simple things, like the technologies we have in our automobiles today to monitor many different systems, balance them, and integrate the operation of those systems, are generally available.

Unfortunately, not much can be done to limit the availability of these technologies. Society expects them and depends on them.

By the same token, the dependence on technology creates vulnerabilities in society. We have a very complicated and inter-dependent infrastructure. One link—one simple change, as we noted in the breakdown in our power grid—can have wide-ranging effects.

Ultimately, what the terrorist is trying to do is create terror. Our job is to try and prevent that terror from spreading. But all too often, because of the interconnection of society, in trying to keep people from panicking, and having them be prepared, we create that panic in and of ourselves.

As I noted, Sun Tzu's statement, "Kill one and terrorize a thousand," is no less applicable today than it was twenty-three hundred years ago. Media and communications have perhaps the single greatest impact in spreading information and data and bringing society together.

In many ways, society is, in fact, more fragile. Technology and the impacts on society have a cascading effect. It's a domino effect, if you will. One thing that occurs spreads throughout all of society. *Small* events have *big* impacts.

Consider the kind of checks that were performed in Washington, D.C. during the time of the snipers in the Fall of 2002. From the point of view of Americans, this was a very startling and very significant change in our society. This had an incredibly significant impact, where one of the most powerful cities in the sole remaining super-power was almost stopped completely for two weeks because of two snipers.

Consider the other impact of small events. In the case of Bhopal, the initiation of that disaster was a relatively small failure in a valve of a chemical processing facility. The end result was a direct physical, medical and health impact on more than five million people; an impact that is still today being felt on society in India.

Consider the growth of telecommunications technology. From 1995 to 2000, the increase has been phenomenal in the use of things like satellite phones, cellular wireless subscribers, and internet voice exchange.

Consider the rate of increase—not just in the U.S. but throughout the world—

in the use of digital technologies. You may remember a few years ago when we had a single satellite failure that affected communications throughout the world. Everything, from relatively minor issues such as not being able to get gasoline at stations in the United States, to significant issues like not being able to exchange medical information overseas—all was the result of a single satellite failure.

But all is not lost. The goal in many, but not all cases of terrorism, is to upset or potentially defeat the United States. Consider that just 25 years ago, the policy of the United States in evaluating the concept of mutually assured destruction, assumed that in a period of one hour there was the possibility of 75 million people dead, the destruction of two-thirds of the industrial capacity of the United States, and 100 cities completely destroyed in a nuclear exchange with the Soviet Union. We assumed that this could potentially occur as a worst-case scenario, and yet, we also assumed that as a nation, we would be able to survive and go back and fight and win a war. Consider the possibility of a terrorist incident even coming close to those numbers or that significant an impact on a society. And yet, we expected to survive. In the United States, the Presidential Succession Act assumed the destruction of 17 layers of command. Seventeen different layers within the United States could have been removed or incapacitated, and we would still have a chain of command and the ability to function as a nation. This is the definition of the resilience of society.

Of the many technologies to combat terrorism—sensors, modeling and simulation, analysis—perhaps the most important is education and intelligence.

The key issue, I believe, in being able to combat terrorism, is no single technology, but the integration of technology to prepare society as a whole to deal with disaster; to train our society—all of the people—how to recognize problems; using technology to educate the public; to improve our infrastructure; to focus on issues such as medical response; and to provide training for professionals.

This applies to the public as well as to security professionals. To be able to combat terrorism, people—humans—are the most important element, and technologies are merely a tool to support them. The focus still must be on innovation, courage, simplicity, and the motivation of our people.

The same applies for technology as well. The different tools, combined with the people, will be much greater than the sum of the individual parts.

I cannot emphasize highly enough that technology, important though it is—and personally I was trained as an engineer and I'm a firm believer in technology—does not replace people. Technology is just a tool to support the people of our society, and we must focus on making technology that better supports our ability as a society to respond. It is vital to support the government, our professionals, and our first responders, but it is even more important to focus on supporting the individuals who are directly affected by terrorism.

We have a great deal of effort and investment being made in things such as detectors, modeling, improved intelligence—the relatively easy problems. What we need to focus on, however, is developing more technologies to train and educate our public, to help exchange information, not just of terrorist events, but of our ability to respond. We need to create a strength, a resilience, a belief in our people, in the technology and our governments and their ability to be able to support and combat terrorism.

In summary, technology is a two-edged sword, for both the terrorists and the anti-terrorists. Work is ongoing in the conventional arena to support the specialists: better sensors, better weapons, better protective systems and improved communications. But we must also focus on how to support the non-specialist—all of the people in society, who, ultimately, are the ones who will be most affected by terrorism, and ultimately, are the ones who will have to respond. Technology is just a tool to support the people and that must be kept in mind.

As a final thought, nothing replaces well-trained, competent, and motivated people. People are the most important asset, and no amount of investment or focus on technology will ever replace that.

Cyber-Terrorism: Evolution and Trends

Dr. Abraham R. Wagner

President, System Research &
Development Corporation, USA

Cyber-Terrorism represents the intersection of two distinct historical phenomena—cybernetics or cyberspace, and terrorism. By one definition, cyberspace is the "virtual world" of symbolic or binary representation of information—that place where computer programs function and data moves. In simpler terms, it is the world of computers and networks. Terrorism is a term used incessantly these days, and for present purposes, we can use the US State Department definition of terrorism as "premeditated, politically motivated violence perpetrated against noncombatant targets by sub-national groups or clandestine agents." Combining these definitions, the result is the following working definition:

Cyber-terrorism is the premeditated, politically motivated attack against information, computer systems, computer programs, and data that result in violence against noncombatant targets by sub-national groups or clandestine agents.

In order for cyber-terrorism to have a unique meaning, it must be differentiated from other kinds of computer-aided abuse such as computer crime, economic espionage, or information warfare.[76] To make this distinction, consider these two phenomena in a little more detail.

Terrorism. To put this phenomenon in perspective, it is useful to consider

---

76 This is an important point. In order to discuss the role of computers with respect to terrorism, we must understand their limits. Short of electrocuting one's self with the power supply or being so unfortunate as to walk under a falling machine, computers cannot, directly, kill or injure. That is not to say that there are not indirect risks of physical harm, nor direct risks of economic injury. Computers may communicate to other devices that do have physical actions that can cause death or injury. The direct risks of economic injury are perhaps the most significant of all the risks. While computers may be referred to as "weapons", they act indirectly.

David Rapoport's excellent historic analysis, tracing the evolution of terrorism in terms of several waves, or cycles, beginning in the late 18th century.[77] Over the years a wide range of groups have used various weapons and tactics against established authorities to achieve various political and social objectives. According to this analysis, we appear to be in a fourth wave of this phenomenon, which is not likely to end anytime soon. Within this current wave we have seen terrorist organizations embrace weapons and techniques they hoped would give them the impact and visibility they desire. We are all well aware of the recent scope of these activities in the Middle East and elsewhere.

Cybernetics. This is a far more recent phenomenon than terrorism, and has developed over the last three decades from a technical curiosity to an entity that affected a fundamental paradigm change with impact on almost all aspects of everyday life. Computers, chips, and networks are clearly everywhere. In terms of actual threats to these technologies and systems, it is possible to bound the problem quickly. At the one end, the little chips that run your watch or permit your auto to start will escape even the best-laid plans of the Hizballah and al Qaida (your Timex will go on ticking…). At the other end, the penultimate apocalypse of cyber-terrorism depicted in films from "War Games" (1983) to the more recent "Terminator 3" is equally unlikely.[78] The real problems are more moderate, and stem from an increasingly computerized and networked world.

There are various accounts of precisely when the cybernetics revolution began, and what were the initial catalytic events.[79] It doesn't really matter much what date is selected. A great deal of this technology revolution came out of work sponsored by the US Defense Department's Advanced Research

---

77 David C. Rapoport, "The Modern History of Terror: The Fourth Wave, Current History", December 2001.

78 Although produced some 20 years apart, both films involved plots where computers controlling the release of US nuclear weapons were taken over by terrorists, or terrorist software, causing an end to the planet. A similar plot is used in "The Net" (1997) that inspired President Clinton to issue PD-63.

79 For a good account, see Stephen Segaller, Nerds 2.0.1: A Brief History of the Internet, New York: TV Books, 1998.

Projects Agency (DARPA). When DARPA started its Cybernetics Technology Office in the mid-1970s, almost nobody had ever heard of the terms cybernetics or cyber space. There was no Internet—only the ARPAnet—and in those days the "net" only connected DARPA's contractors and associates at the universities and elsewhere. The worldwide web wasn't even a part of the ARPAnet vision. Local area network (LAN) technology, developed in Palo Alto at the Xerox research center, under DARPA contract, was scorned by the Xerox corporate management, who could not conceive it would ever be useful for anything.[80] For their part, the esteemed trustees of Stanford University thought the development of the router, by Len Bohack at Stanford under yet another DARPA contract, to be equally useless.[81] In short, it would have been difficult to imagine a real cyber-terrorist scenario in those days. The net impact would have been "zero." Temporarily cutting off some contractor or professor from his DARPA sponsor would have no visibility and would have caused little damage. Indeed, it would have hardly gotten any coverage in *The New York Times*, and in those days CNN did not yet exist.

To understand how the problem evolved, it is useful to consider a few key elements of this technical revolution:

"Moore's Law" named after Gordon Moore, co-founder of Intel and inventor of the integrated circuit, states that the number of transistors on a single chip will double about every two years, with the result being increasingly cheap and powerful integrated circuits (chips).[82] This is rapidly becoming the era

---

80 The inventors of the LAN soon left X-PARC to found the 3-COM Corporation.

81 Shortly thereafter Len and his wife Sandy Bohack left Stanford to found CISCO in their garage on Oak Grove Avenue in Menlo Park.

82 The numbers behind Moore's Law are illustrated below:

	Year of introduction	Transistors
4004	1971	2,250
8008	1972	2,500
8080	1974	5,000
8086	1978	29,000
286	1982	120,000
386ª processor	1985	275,000
486ª DX processor	1989	1,180,000
Pentium™ processor	1993	3,100,000

of virtually free hardware. For the first time in the history of mankind, the marginal cost of high technology is approaching zero. The impact of this phenomenon should not be underestimated.

Packet Switching. What began in the 1960's as an MIT doctoral dissertation by Leonard Klienrock, and shortly appeared thereafter as an IEEE paper by Vincent Cerf and Robert Kahn has become a worldwide technical and economic reality. It is simply a lot more efficient than the line switching, which has existed for close to two centuries. At the time, nobody would have predicted that this technology would soon usher in the largest media revolution since the invention of moveable type.

Digital Everything. it doesn't matter what "it" is, it is now digital—voice, data, video, pictures. This phenomenon is really quite astonishing, since it is a great deal more than a technological revolution; it is a social and cultural revolution as well. Indeed, few would have predicted that the culture of business, personal lives, government and the military all would have moved this quickly to embrace the new technology.

Infinite/cheap Bandwidth. in both RF and landline (fiber optic) the cost of bandwidth continues to fall, and availability continues to grow worldwide. We are still trying to learn the real economics of the new forms of communications, but for all practical purposes the decrease in cost has enabled access for a large segment of the world's population. New access technologies (e.g., web-enabled cell phones, laptops, Wi-Fi, etc.) continue to proliferate.

Over the past three decades, these developments have brought the world to the point where possible cyber-attacks really do matter. The net result of all this, for better or worse, has been movement at an astonishing pace from an analog world to a digital one dominated by interconnected systems, for communications, information, control, finance, and national security. There has been not only a technological revolution, but a social and cultural one as well. On the one hand, these systems provide great efficiencies and

Pentium II processor	1997	7,500,000
Pentium III processor	1999	24,000,000
Pentium 4 processor	2000	42,000,000

capabilities; on the other they create potential vulnerabilities. The real questions of cyber-terrorism are just what vulnerabilities this creates; what can be done about the problem; and by whom.

In looking at the issues of cyber-terrorism, it is essential to bear in mind that this form of terrorism differs from others in that both the weapons and the targets are highly dynamic in nature. Virtually all other forms of terrorist activity are highly static, in that the weapons and the targets really don't change very much from year to year. Looking at the "classic" terrorist targets and weapons:

Crowded markets have been around for millennia; crowded buses for almost a century.

Tall buildings have been with us for over a century (New York's original "skyscraper"—the Flatiron Building, was constructed in 1902, and even the World Trade Center, lost in the 9/11 tragedy, was some 30 years old).

Airports haven't changed a great deal, in technical terms, in over 50 years, and train stations in probably over 100. The addition of guards and metal detectors is the only recent advancement.

Tunnels and bridges have been around for centuries, and even the "new" technology here is decades old.

Military camps date back to biblical times, even though tents are now more modern and air-conditioned.

Bombs and explosives date back centuries, and the "recent" invention of such things as plastic explosives is decades old.

Rifles and automatic weapons also date back a century or more.

In the cyber world the story is much different, with the technology changing to a "new generation" every 18 months, by some analyses. While this number may be a little suspect, it is clear that the target environment is highly dynamic and "weapons" developed to attack must be constantly upgraded or replaced to work at all. Being an effective cyber terrorist requires a serious, ongoing development program. Much of the government's failure in this area, discussed at some length below, has also been for this reason, i.e. a lack of appreciation for the dynamics of the situation and the need for an ongoing development effort.

Current and Future Trends

There is no stopping the technical revolution; none of the aforementioned technical trends is likely to abate in the foreseeable future. Computers and related hardware will continue to grow cheaper and more powerful. Hybrid devices "connected" to the world will continue to proliferate at an escalating rate. These technologies are too cost-effective, and bring about all sorts of wonderful capabilities. Private citizens, business and the government (including the military) are all addicted. The real questions are the extent to which business, commerce, government, and national security depend on systems that are vulnerable, and whether these vulnerabilities can be addressed.

The convenience of remote access to information has led the commercial world to rush headlong into reliance on the World Wide Web, a form of information access that did not exist a decade ago. This growing information medium was grafted onto a network that was not initially designed for this type of utilization and therefore benefited little from attention to security. Traditional, brute force security techniques, such as physically isolating secure systems have limited applicability in a world where immediate access to multiple information sources is essential. The decentralized nature of the Internet and the technical nature of existing network protocols provide network reliability and scalability but complicate security.

At the same time, there is good news for at least two reasons. The first is that the technology is really asymmetrical.[83] Technology and economics really do favor the defense, and over time it will become increasingly difficult and costly, if not impossible, to attack computers and other elements of the net. Hardware and software "fixes" to various vulnerabilities are being developed and implemented on an ongoing basis. Security vulnerabilities now receive

---

83 Compare this to the experience of the development of radar, and radar countermeasures; submarines and ASW technology; and more recently to low-observable (stealth) and counter-stealth technology. All are really asymmetric.

a great deal of publicity when identified, and "patches" are quickly and freely made available over the net. Increasingly, computers are being configured to check the net for updates on a regular basis without user intervention. Hacking is really getting harder.

Second, and equally important, is that this is a technology we understand, and we are in a position to provide relatively cost-effective technical solutions. The technology came from DARPA—not Pakistan or Iraq. Why the US and other industrial nations have thus far failed to provide better solutions lies with both government and industry failings. In the pre-9/11 era these problems were addressed in Presidential Directive PD-63, as well as military exercises in 1998, but the incentive to "cure" the problems was not there. In the post 9/11 world, the incentives are far stronger and the prospects greater. Preventing cyber-terrorism is much less of a technology problem, than one of economics and national will. Unlike drug interdiction and a few other areas where government actions are largely hopeless, this is an area where the problems can be solved.

What is the real threat in this area?

At the present time there is significant debate over the threat of cyber-terrorism. Various writings on both sides of this issue are contained in the *References* section of this paper below. It is unfortunate that many of those involved in the debate, including government officials, military personnel, and journalists, have limited or no real technical expertise and are commenting on matters they simply don't understand.[84] In part, the discussion arises because some people see the two relatively disjointed phenomena (terrorism and cybernetics) and think they must logically intersect at some point. Leaving aside Hizballah and al Qaida for a moment, who have been the major attackers of the net?

Hackers: To date, the vast majority of all cyber attacks have come from "hackers" of several types. These range from bored high-school kids to those depicted in the film *The Matrix*. In most cases, hackers are best described as malicious, but not actually terrorists. They seek neither money nor the end of

---

84 It is equally fortunate that they are not practicing medicine where they could do even more harm.

the US (or Israeli) government. For a number of reasons they just get perverse pleasure from annoying others.

Criminals: Since commerce, banks etc. have increasingly moved to computers and networks, it is only natural that criminals have moved to this venue as well. Since a group of Russian cyber criminals attacked New York's City Bank several years ago, commercial firms have gotten a great deal more interested in protecting their systems from criminal penetration.

Disgruntled employees: Statistically, a large number of problems we see these days come from former employees (e.g., system administrators) who are angry with their employers, not the nation.

What has not been seen thus far are any significant efforts on the part of a major terrorist group to attack these systems. Further, there is little evidence thus far of a technology base or sophisticated development program in this area among any terrorist group that can even rival the average high school student in America. US intelligence, military and law enforcement officers have captured computers and hardware from all sorts of terrorists worldwide, and the conclusion one can draw is that they are users of the Internet and not attackers of the Internet. This is not to say the situation won't change, but these are the data that exist to date.

Computers and networked systems provide capability, and terrorists have for some time recognized this and utilized these capabilities to further their own ends. When this was suggested by several outside experts to the leaders of the US Intelligence Community in the early 1980's, they were largely ignored and laughed at. Now that Internet cafes, AOL, yahoo, and hotmail have become the terrorists' preferred means of communication, they are laughing a great deal less, and paying significantly more attention to the problem.

Speaking at the Council on Foreign Relations in 1998, John Hamre, then Deputy Secretary of Defense, discussed national security concerns arising from the globalization of technology. He recounted the results of an exercise called "ELIGIBLE RECEIVER." A "Red Team" of some 35 computer experts from the National Security Agency were given three months to plan and execute an electronic attack on DoD information systems and on elements of the national infrastructure that support DoD. Using only public

Internet access and commonly available hardware and software, the Red Team demonstrated that it could untraceably "bring down" the telecommunications system that is the backbone of DoD command and control, as well as a major portion of national electric power grids and 911 systems. Although they only gained "root access" to 36 of the 40,000 Pentagon network servers they interrogated, this was assessed to be enough to have prevented the command and control system from operating effectively to support a deployment.

Evidence like this must be viewed in perspective. First, ELIGIBLE RECEIVER was undertaken some five years ago—at least two net generations past. Second, almost three dozen NSA technical experts were employed—a resource no terrorist group is likely to have access to. Finally, this group only gained access to a minute fraction of the DoD computers interrogated, and the vulnerabilities that permitted this type of root access have long since been eliminated.

More recently (2002) an exercise held at the Naval War College called "DIGITAL PEARL HARBOR" using a group of outside experts concluded that a terrorist cyber-attack was possible, but would require a $200-million investment and five years to accomplish. Again, these are US experts possibly applying DoD concepts of program management and funding. Presumably a terrorist organization could undertake a less costly program, but it still suggests the magnitude of the problem.

Still, significant concerns remain about abilities to defend against a cyber attack. Several widely publicized incidents—including the takeover of the *New York Times* web site by a hacker group and the compromise of the Stanford University e-mail system—have at least raised the level of public concern. The Fall 1998 issue if the National Academy of Science's *Issues in Science and Technology* contains two articles offering opposing assessments of the real extent of infrastructure vulnerability to cyber attack, and the October 1998 *Scientific American* has a special report on "How Hackers Break In."

As this example shows, information warfare defense overlaps with critical infrastructure protection. An ability to defend critical infrastructure against cyber attack is important to protect the United States against this new form of strategic attack. At a less grand level, defense of the commercial infrastructure is important to ensure the continued operation of DoD communications and information systems that largely rely on commercial infrastructure. DoD needs to ensure that its own combat and supporting communications and information systems, many of which are built from commercial (COTS) software and hardware components can be defended against cyber attack.

Looking to the threat to the business world, commercial firms face a variety of threats that have various motivations. There are hackers who merely want a challenge, but who may inadvertently damage a system or expose confidential information in the process. Competitors may use information attacks for commercial espionage, looking for corporate R&D, marketing or financial secrets, or even seeking to disrupt corporate operations. Disgruntled present or former employees or customers may attempt sabotage, destroying data or bringing a transaction processing system to a halt. These motivations and types of threats generally overlap with those of immediate concern to the government for its own information systems. In its role as a purchaser, the government has many of the aspects of a commercial participant in the marketplace. In protecting information on troop movements or R&D secrets, the government has an interest in defeating computer-based espionage and disruption. Clearly the government and military are attractive targets for hackers.

The most commonly mentioned commercial security concern is pecuniary— theft of money through bogus financial transactions, or theft of services (for example, by cloning cellular phone codes). The consensus is that such mischief cost the US some $15-billion last year. At first blush, this financial threat motivation has only a limited analog in the national security area, often leading commentators to suggest that there is a radical difference between commercial and government security concerns. But increasingly, the government as a participant in the electronic marketplace will have an immediate concern with these issues, as well as a law enforcement concern for minimizing the level of civilian crime.

Many experts have been concerned about some nonchalance in the commercial world concerning theft. Financial institutions that have been the victims of computer theft often have a motive to prevent this information from becoming public, as it might hurt their stock price and reputation among potential depositors and clients. Especially in new industries, where firms are trying to capture market share for the future, and especially in industries (such as telecom or cable television) with a low or zero marginal cost of service, some level of theft of services may be tolerated, at least for a while. Clearly if the same sort of security flaw could be exploited to gain crucial national security information leading to the loss of life, then DoD could not accept typical commercial practices as its own standard of information protection.

Nevertheless, looking toward the future, it seems likely that commercial practices for information security will improve. Once new industries get beyond the steep phase of their growth curve, firms become much more conscious of revenue. Means of theft once exploited by the few become widespread and thus too expensive to tolerate. Computer security has become a recognized specialty of a variety of firms. The explosive growth of the information industry has produced other effects that further militate against high levels of information assurance. Immature technology and commercial incentives to beat rivals to market have produced many unnecessary vulnerabilities in commercial systems and software, and limited US technical labor supplies have led US firms, including government suppliers to employ programmers in foreign countries not allied with the US.

There are no magic wands to deal with these problems. As the industry matures, security will increasingly be a selling point for hardware, software, and service providers. As commerce relies increasingly on secure information flows, the private stakes associated with computer security will rise. At the same time, with the emergence of the next-generation Internet, there is the potential to replace the current, jury-rigged, system with one that has security designed in from the start.

With this general background, it is possible to consider three national security concerns and see how they may place different demands on capabilities for defending against cyber attack.

Strategic societal vulnerability. Defects in commercial systems could create a strategic opportunity for an enemy to threaten, or actually inflict damage on, our society. Most of these defects would be exploitable for pecuniary gain or for revenge against a particular company, and so would be a focus of commercial information assurance efforts. Over time, concerns for private liability should make private utilities and firms adopt a higher standard of security.

At the same time, the government may still have a higher level of concern than private firms. For example, attempts to bring a network down through congestion might not be elegant enough to be interesting to hackers, but might still be effective in the hands of a foreign power or cyber terrorist. More dangerous are likely to be known vulnerabilities that are simply not plugged by less vigilant sectors of the economy, such as the electric utilities targeted in ELIGIBLE RECEIVER.

Despite attempts through the President's Commission on Critical Infrastructure Protection, and now Presidential Decision Directive 63, many sectors of private industry have been reluctant to share information on their vulnerabilities and on how to deal with them. The problem is complicated by the increasing fractionation of utilities and transport industries through deregulation, and by the increasing internationaliтation of telecommunications, finance, oil, and other key infrastructure firms. Former national security officials Ash Carter, John Deutch, and Philip Zelikow suggest, in an article in *Foreign Affairs,* the formation of a non-profit public-private organization that would do red-teaming and provide information-sharing and consulting services to critical infrastructure enterprises. Such an organization could also serve as a trusted dissemination mechanism for government warnings, changes in threat conditions, and appropriate defensive responses.

Government dependence on commercial infrastructure. A terrorist group or other enemy could target commercial communications systems in the US and elsewhere to interfere with the more than 90% of government communications that are normally supplied commercially. Similarly, an enemy might attempt to disrupt a deployment by inducing a power blackout or air-traffic control outage in areas surrounding points of embarkation. Such attacks could be more discriminating than strategic attacks but still have operationally important consequences. Even a temporary success could have significant value. The typical hacker, disgruntled employee, or thief will typically not be interested in creating even this level of disruption, for fear of the consequences. Thus even this sort of attack might take advantage of vulnerability modes not typically of major concern to the private sector. The same sorts of public-private cooperation that is needed to deal with strategic vulnerabilities can be useful here as well.

Government use of commercial (COTS) hardware and software in its combat and support information systems and networks. The dramatic improvement in both performance and cost gained from using systems and software written for commercial purposes has led the US Defense Department to reduce its earlier insistence that software be written to DoD specifications. In general, DoD relies on commercial systems and software for its networked computer systems. While the most sensitive and classified systems can be kept secure through special measures (such as physical isolation and very high levels of surveillance), many other DoD systems exhibit the same sorts of vulnerabilities that are prevalent in commercial systems. Moreover, high civilian salaries have limited the government's ability to hire and retain the most qualified personnel for systems administration, and system security has not always had the highest priority in the rush to take advantage of the new information technology. Right now, DoD use of open systems together with wide knowledge of the vulnerabilities of these systems is a major cause for concern.

The banking and finance industry already incorporates formidable security into its electronic infrastructure. As electronic banking, commerce, and critical data storage become more widespread, their associated security technologies will permeate national systems, including many of those used by DoD. These security technologies will feature the best the commercial world has to offer in firewalls, intrusion response systems, malicious code detection, and encryption. Furthermore, good security practices and awareness will develop alongside the incorporation of these technologies (many best practices are already supposed to be incorporated into DoD system administration). These trends will help ensure that the commercial networks that support DoD and other national security functions will be robust against most efforts of cyber attack.

Good practices at the level of the individual computer or network need to be supplemented by a synoptic view of security at the system-of-systems level. The addition of new systems to the infrastructure can increase the level of threat to the existing nodes. One-time certification procedures do not adequately account for the fact that infrastructures are dynamic, quasi-organic systems. Frequent probing may be required to assess real-world security. Network design should also incorporate redundancy and reconstitution mechanisms, to assure continuity of operations in the event of attack. Such mechanisms would minimize the impact of local failure on the larger infrastructure.

Thus, for the future, as commercial security standards and practices improve, and perhaps as the government outsources more of its information support in an intelligent way, DoD use of commercial standards could become a source of strength. As the commercial market matures, many more resources will be put into computer security (and many more attempts will be made to break it) than would ever have been possible for DoD-unique systems, leading to a more robust security regime. Government-only systems would tend to have more flaws. Even if the flaws were known to fewer potential opponents and thus might be less likely to be exploited, they would be much more vulnerable to traditional espionage (for example, an insider selling information to an enemy) than the commercial systems are likely to be.

Over time, the use of open systems has the potential to become a strength, rather than a weakness. National security systems will, however, always face threats and consequences for failure that are somewhat different from those of the commercial world. Thus the government will need to maintain an active vulnerability assessment and mitigation effort, probably using some combination of specialized government resources and trusted contractors.

Finally, the government's role as a major purchaser of computer and network equipment, software, and services gives it an opportunity to influence the commercial market, even as its direct share of development for information technology declines. The Office of Management and Budget, together with DoD and the other major departments, can act to ensure that continued government-sponsored R&D on computer security fosters commercial innovation, but also that government purchases help encourage the commercial availability of advanced security features.

Strategic Threat Assessment. Traditional threat assessment methods evaluate hostile military capabilities and intent against friendly weaknesses. As ELIGIBLE RECEIVER suggests, a terrorist group or other hostile force may not need significant investment, long-term development and acquisition cycles, or readily observable testing and deployments to achieve a meaningful capability. Such a capability can be achieved using cheap, widely available and easily obtained technology employed in ways that are difficult to trace.

Naturally, threat assessment in this environment tends to be done on the basis of a worst-case assessment of how a clever enemy might exploit our known vulnerabilities. Beyond war games and red teams, it may be possible to deploy decoy targets or software-based search modules in cyberspace that watch out for patterns of probing for vulnerabilities. Such efforts could help better characterize actual methods available to—or being prepared for use—by cyber attackers, helping network and system administrators to better prepare for specific sorts of threats.

It may also be possible to focus attention on the cyberspace activities of foreign forces thought to be hostile to the United States. Intelligence agencies can assess (if imperfectly) the motivations of various foreign powers and non-state actors, and can assess the native cyber resources of these potential threats. They can watch for efforts to recruit or train hackers, or to secure advanced information on computer and network security. They may be able to focus on foreign information attack forces, localizing their means of access to the global information infrastructure and methods of attack. After all, any serious attacking force is unlikely to try to attack out of the blue without any previous preparation. The challenge of finding signatures of such preparations and then gaining access to their substance is likely to be difficult, but not impossible. Having developed this information, both prevention and pre-emption may become possible.

Tactical Warning. Good security technologies and practices can minimize vulnerabilities. However, these vulnerabilities will not be eliminated by the passive application of technology. Human error, sloppy security practices, and even assistance by inside personnel, can allow unauthorized access to the technologically most sophisticated systems. Thus, good security practice at the system and network level will continue to include "red team" attempts to crack our own systems, and also the auditing of access to sensitive parts of the system (such as password files) and surveillance for unusual access attempts or patterns of resource use.

It is important that the results of such surveillance be collated and reported through a warning network that includes both government and private systems administrators. There are two reasons for this. First, since surveillance is likely to be imperfect, and somewhat episodic, a warning that something is happening elsewhere will trigger more focused attention at other sites. For this reason, government dissemination of heightened possibility of information attack cued by other sorts of warning indicators (such as changes in the international political environment or the advent of key anniversaries) may also be important. Second, one of the key techniques of securing unauthorized access to a computer is first to take over a system that is "trusted" by the target. Thus warning of an attempt at access should be propagated though the network of computers that have these trust relationships, so that greater attention can be devoted to similar attempts on other connected machines. The sensitivity of this warning network should be increased during periods when collateral indications (such as other hostile acts or preparations) indicate the potential for a greater threat of cyber attack.

Attack Assessment. Whether or not we manage to obtain advance warning of a cyber attack, we will need a capability for rapid attack detection and assessment. A serious cyber attack typically requires substantial advance probing and intelligence preparation of the (information) battlefield. A sensitive network surveillance system that picks up the early phases of a cyber attack campaign will perhaps provide enough warning to allow defenses to be deployed to blunt the damaging part of the attack. Even if we do not achieve this sort of warning (for example, if the attacker manages to stay below the threshold of notice), attack assessment is important for a technical response and system reconstitution, and also for national security decisions beyond the realm of cyber warfare. The aim of attack assessment is to identify and quantify the nature of attack, source of attack, scope, objective, and strategy of attack, and to shed light on the identity and capabilities of the attacker.

There is no guarantee that defenders will be able to determine the nature and scope of an attack underway: namely whether the information attack is an isolated incident or simple crime, an operation within a coordinated information warfare strategy, or mere accident or incompetence. Questions regarding source of attack and identity of attacker will determine who has jurisdiction for response, as well as the appropriate response. Adversaries could use the purposeful anonymity of cyber attacks to mislead authorities as to the source of the attack, resulting in operational confusion and paralysis.

If early warning fails, then networks themselves may be down or corrupted, and they may not be able to provide detailed information on the attack. A serious adversary might accompany a cyber attack on critical infrastructure with other physical and electronic attacks that might impede assessment and response. If they remain intact, warning and attack assessment mechanisms might assist in identifying attack strategies and objectives. Such assessment requires the collation of detailed information that may not otherwise be retained automatically in network systems, together with systematic assessment of other information, including attack patterns, number of systems affected, nature and commonalities of systems affected, patterns of effects on infrastructures, and activity in other more traditional security areas. The US currently lacks a capability for such a detailed and overall assessment of a serious cyber attack.

What has been done on the private and government levels, and what should be done?

The point of departure for what is to be done is really the changed relation between private and government efforts in the area of information security. In the past, the government had much greater technical resources and investments in communications and computer security than did the private sector. The balance is shifting to the point that, aside from some unique government needs and concerns, the commercial sector will be dominant in the development of information assurance technologies and services. Thus the increasing government reliance on commercial systems and services means that the government activities in information protection will build on an increasingly sophisticated commercial infrastructure. The issue of defense against cyber attack can thus be simplified by understanding where commercial and government concerns and capabilities may diverge. From this, one can focus government efforts on areas where the market is unlikely to provide an adequate solution.

In all fairness, it is not possible to accurately forecast the threat in this area, and we need to prepare. In passing, let me move on the final set of comments, and report on efforts undertake by the US Government in this area in the past several years.

DD-63 (National Infrastructure Protection). At Vice President Gore's urging, President Clinton signed a Presidential Directive that at least focused some attention on the issue of infrastructure vulnerability. By one account, Clinton saw the movie "The Net" and became worried about the possible problem. In any case, the Presidential Directive did give rise to a Presidential Commission, and some study of the problem. The results of their work got mixed reviews, but led to the establishment of the National Infrastructure Protection Center (NIPC) at the FBI and a few developments—not all bad. Without digressing into a discussion of what was done right and wrong in this exercise, it is possible to suggest that the US Government was not urged to do a great deal, largely out of Vice President Gore's personal conviction that when "industry" saw the true nature of their vulnerability, they would leap into the breach and fix the problems. Gore did not focus on the fact that industry was far more concerned with quarter-to-quarter profits than potential vulnerabilities to cyber attacks.

GII (Global Information Infrastructure). During his tenure as DCI, Dr. John Deutch asked a group of internal and outside experts to take a far-ranging look at the evolution of the worldwide "global information infrastructure" and see what problems and opportunities were presented. After some two years of work and research, very little resulted in significant changes or programs.

DARPA and the CERT. On the plus side, some years ago, DARPA initiated the Computer Emergency Response Team (CERT) at Carnegie-Mellon University, where it had available an extremely bright and capable group of computer scientists to provide a national 911 capability for network emergencies. Over the years, the effort has expanded and been replicated in a number of countries, and stands as one good example of how to prepare for future emergencies and cyber attacks.

NIPC. The FBI's National Infrastructure Protection Center (NIPC) represents the nation's current early warning capability, but it still lacks most of the reporting and monitoring mechanisms, the intelligence support, and the Federal interagency integration that a fully effective early warning capability would require. Another national capability envisioned by PDD-63, the Information Sharing and Analysis Center (ISAC), offers a national-level monitoring capability integrating government agencies and the private sector. However, this Center exists largely on paper, and would not provide a reactive or real-time monitoring capability for effective early warning. As suggested in the next sections, early warning must be integrated with attack assessment, technical response and reconstitution.

The passive defenses of network security and information assurance are the crucial platform on which to build an information warfare defense capability. However, the appearance of sophisticated cyber threats will require an active, consolidated system that integrates capabilities for warning, attack assessment, response, and reconstitution across the government/commercial divide.

Cyber-defense is unlikely to require the level of effort that went into nuclear weapons in the 1950's. The problems of providing an effective warning and response capability are nevertheless similar. The US invested great sums in strategic intelligence and contemporaneous warning capabilities, attack assessment, and secure response capabilities, in an attempt to ensure continuity of government and essential services. The government worried about ensuring an ability to attribute the source of an attack. Deterrence is less relevant to cyber attack than to nuclear attack, but it should not be ruled completely off the table.

In the context of cyber attack and information warfare, detailed threat assessment and strategic warning may be an insurmountable challenge. Incidents—electronic and physical—will happen. The need for detection and containment of an attack is quickly emerging as a requirement for policy and operational attention that is as important as deterrence and protection. Early warning and attack assessment capabilities developed for the North American Air Defense Command (NORAD) at Cheyenne Mountain during the Cold War offer at least an analogy for consideration.

In a digital-era NORAD, rapid warning, response, and reconstitution capabilities would have to extend deep into the commercial sphere, and would require effective cooperation among Federal agencies and between the public and private sectors. The NIPC is at least a model of such cooperation in the context of PDD-63. Such centers do not, however, yet go beyond cooperation on planning, and do not address how the public and private sector can work together in early warning detection, assessment, containment of cyber attacks, and reconstitution.

Conclusion

On balance, the response of the US Government to the evolving threat can best be described as very little, very late. In some cases, US policy can only be described as silly. Indeed, a national policy that seeks to place export controls on software and data that is already freely available on the worldwide web makes no sense. Similarly, placing export controls on hardware that are already on the world market serve no useful purpose, and only serve to harm the balance of trade. Certainly such actions impede no foreign power or terrorist. One can only hope that the current administration takes a somewhat more realistic approach.

Even at DARPA, cradle of the cybernetics revolution, with an annual budget on the order of $2.7 billion, the investment in cyber-defense has been exceedingly small, and until very recently was largely limited to CERT. The organization that gave rise to the net saw little need to protect or defend it, despite the "D" getting added back into their name.

For its part, the US Intelligence Community has not distinguished itself. While the details are still protected under the cloak of secrecy, the history is highly embarrassing. How well the Intelligence Community and the DoD can play "catch up" is still an open question.

In the final analysis, do the terrorists really care? Will a cyber attack give them the sort of visibility and destruction they are looking for? Are they willing to invest in the technical capability to pull one off? It is a radically different technology than some young terrorist wrapped in explosives who self-destructs on a bus or in a crowded marketplace.

On the other hand, will the commercial sector pre-empt government action and make such cyber attacks increasingly difficult? Network operators and communications providers continue to add security features and layers of protection. The net itself is inherently survivable—a characteristic of packet switching. The infrastructure is one without a single point of failure.

Responding to Post-Modern Terrorism

Containment of a Mega Terrorism Attack

Amb. Dr. Jon Glassman

Vice President, Northrop Grumman Electronic
Systems, International, United States

Today I will address mega-terrorism in terms of the outcome, rather than the means. In the course of this symposium we have heard repeatedly that the target of terrorism is not the dead, i.e. the victims, but rather the people who live—the terrorists' own constituencies in the Muslim world, or the threatened populations, meaning the Americans, Israelis and Europeans. Therefore, the counter terrorists' target must also be the living.

My definition of mega terrorism is an event whose outcome requires complex, extraordinary responses involving multiple organizations. So today, terrorism will be discussed as a managerial challenge–a challenge involving intricate orchestration and management in order to turn this cacophony of multiple actors and responders into a harmonious symphony.

Now, what does it take to orchestrate this symphony? Primarily, it necessitates a group of people who are empowered to take command in terrorist incidents, and not just one particular incident, but all incidents. A leadership must be designated beforehand to handle management. In addition, a modular organizational structure is mandatory. Even now, in Iraq, it is clear that the American military is reorganizing units in new combinations. For instance, deployment in the field will involve a battalion of infantry soldiers accompanied by some civil affairs soldiers, administrative staff, and maybe some psy-ops experts. A new unit will be created by assembling modules. American responses and units require reconstruction.

It is essential to have resources that can be moved to the scene of the incident or incidents. Most importantly, a technological infrastructure, an IT infrastructure, enabling the introduction of certain processes, is vital. A common picture is needed to reflect the situation; this entails imagery. An accurate description of the situation is crucial to collaborative planning and analysis, and ensures that everyone is reading from the same page. Cross-organizational communication is imperative; when a military unit arrives, along with a police unit and the fire brigade, they can all communicate with each other, thus allowing a planned, systematic execution of tasks.

Counter-terrorism is composed of several stages. The first stage consists of intelligence, preventive action and warnings prior to events. The next phase is when an actual incident occurs. This involves management of the immediate crisis, usually handled by the police and the military. Consequence management is necessary, i.e., resuscitation and evacuation of victims to hospitals. Lastly comes the stage of possible retaliation and political management of the incident. Often people tend to focus on the front end. That is to say, the intelligence entities do their work, and then other forces handle the situation. I submit that this is faulty practice. What is needed is an end-to-end operation, an application of capabilities across the phases. An operation, if you will, that conveys a message of counter-terrorism's competence and dominance.

Part of the message, in addition to framing and discussing the correct terminology and concepts, is how to cope with terrorism. A terrorist incident must be handled successfully in order to prove that disorder does not prevail. We must convey the message that we are capable of handling anything. If we can transmit this image repeatedly, over time, we will emerge triumphant.

The situation is as follows: A terrorist organization chooses a target or technique. The terrorist event is perpetrated, and is then followed by a series of responses. The terrorists have the initiative at the front end, but the initiative in the back end is ours. The obvious preliminary goal is to eliminate the terrorists' options up front, or to prevent the action if possible. If this cannot be done, then efforts should focus on acquiring some evidence as to the terrorists' possible plans. At this stage, attempts are made to mitigate the attack, or at least contain the damage that it may inflict. Then, ultimately, it is important to control the political message that emerges from the event, both in words and actions (including retaliation). It is essential to maintain control over the response, so that the latter is handled in the best possible and orderly manner.

Regarding pre-event requirements, we in the intelligence business, understand our tasks; the terrorists must be detected or tracked, their plans understood, their actions prevented, and the consequences mitigated. This becomes an interesting point, because rarely is full knowledge available, and in some cases the terrorist act cannot be completely prevented. But if partial knowledge is available regarding the technique and the location of the threat, some of the consequences can be mitigated. How do we learn about these people and how do we obtain these facts? The first stage is obvious to anyone in the intelligence business. There is human intelligence, imagery, etc. Analysis can be conducted, based on currently available databases, or databases which can be created through tracking people. An organization like SITA, for example, has access to all air records, as well as car rental and hotel records, which can be useful. But the issue is to try to use this data as we proceed and to analyze case after case, to develop diverse *modus operandi* and various scenarios from which terrorist behavior emerges.

We need to study identification using diverse biometrics. On my El Al flight to Israel, I noticed that they were very careful to examine my passport and scan my little briefcase for explosives, but I saw no one validating whether I was really the person in my passport. There was no biometric authentication. This must be remedied. It is vital to search for and correlate data from diverse intelligence and law enforcement organizations, both domestically and internationally. In my work overseas I have noted that different security organizations do not share information; the military does not share information with the police. This situation, where there is no cross-fertilization, must change. Additionally, analyst collaboration is vital. The method should be to generate possible threat scenarios, perform risk analyses vis-à-vis the possible target, and provide options for dealing with the situation.

This is the picture that emerges from Total Information, or the Terrorism Information Awareness Program in the US that was not funded by Congress for privacy reasons. In that program, transactional data were studied, as well as biometric data. The objective was to collaborate analytically.

Once it becomes possible to acquire all of these resources and databases, and all the involved parties enable cross-fertilization, a multi-intelligence operations center can be created. Those of you who are in the military know that these centers exist for targeting, for fire control. This type of center must be duplicated within the counter-terrorism world. On this basis, link analysis must be conducted between individuals and groups, and scenarios must be hypothesized vis-à-vis how events may develop. These elements must be integrated within an alert structure, incorporating threat locations and techniques, real-time analytical exchanges, and shared assessments. Most important is the element of dissemination with multi-level security. Obviously, if sensitive human intelligence is acquired it must be kept confidential. Methods must be generated to sanitize information and create alerts, so that the involved parties understand what they are required to do, especially the first responders. Among other things, this will enable mitigation of the threat.

In other words, if, for example, we know a particular technique is going to be used, or if we have pinpointed a location, there are certain geo-spatial products that can be produced. We can observe the topography and talk about access routes for emergency vehicles. We can discuss visualization by tilting a building model or schematic to analyze access. We can also study the internal spaces of buildings, in case of emergency. Floor plans and internal photos are available, so that the decision makers and people who have to act are provided with the tools to mitigate or respond to the threat.

To conclude this section, this process is currently under implementation in the US Department of Homeland Security. A strategic analysis of the enemy is received and is combined with an analysis of particular threats and vulnerability assessments of locations. These elements are incorporated in a mapping function, enabling warning and protective action.

As I just mentioned, in terms of mitigating the threat, a means for rapid processing and sanitizing of information is imperative. If vital information cannot be circulated or processed into a coherent warning, then it is totally useless to the people who must protect their location. So this process needs to be launched immediately. As indicated, data and imagery support for possible target areas are essential. If there exists whole or partial knowledge of the target or technique, we can plan evacuations, redeployment of potential responders, and prepare medication and personal protective equipment if chemical or biological incidents are anticipated, etc. When addressing post-event activities, two elements are classically mentioned. One is the response to the immediate crisis via law-enforcement forces and the police, while the other is the restoration of services.

The concept that these are two separate issues, that there are people who do intelligence work and then walk away from the scene, must be avoided. This is a dynamic process, in which intelligence must continue to be linked to a supreme operational controller of the event.

What happened during 9/11 and some previous large-scale disasters? It is evident that there was limited sharing of intelligence; there were numerous stovepipe organizations, poor command and control between various civilian authorities and the military, as well as a piecemeal response—all under a vertical command structure; entities reported only to their superiors. This chain-of-command structure, which is prevalent in the New York police and the FBI, must be revised. Confusion reigned due to the number of agencies involved, each with its own particular jurisdictional mandate. This type of scene cannot be approached with confusion. Each entity must be aware of its role upon arrival. Response must not involve ad-hoc coordination of the command relations at the scene, piecemeal commitment of response resources, and the lack of a viable plan. To date, each agency has acted only according to its own communications protocols, its own feedback and its own hierarchical structure. To add to the confusion, in many cases physical communications are actually interrupted. This is what occurred during 9/11 and on other occasions. This, then, is the key, which must be put in place before incidents occur: a system must exist—a pre-established hierarchy of authority—for handling these types of crises, both in general, and at the scene of the incident.

In the United States, there is some movement in this direction, in the form of a Federal Response Plan. The FBI is assigned the lead upon the occurrence of a terrorist act. In other countries different organizations may be in charge, but there must be one entity that will assume authority, as well as a mechanism for tailoring the nature and the scale of the response. This entails a prior division of labor among agencies. According to the United States Federal Response Plan, each of those functions is handed to a Cabinet Department. Thus, when arriving at the scene of an emergency, each Cabinet Departments knows that it is obligated to handle a specific function once the federal government is involved. The allocation of roles is arranged in advance and is known to all of the involved parties, thus avoiding enormous confusion.

What would happen, for example, in the event of a sarin attack? What would happen if the EOD Brigade arrived, in addition to the navy commandos and so forth? The result would be chaos. It is a known fact that in Israel, the police are in charge. That agency will handle these tasks so that there will be no confusion.

Further to the matter of imagery and database support, when dealing with a weapon of mass destruction, a good staging area, as well as a triage and a decontamination area, must all be prepared. The topography must be studied. For example, in which direction might contaminated water flow; what direction is the wind blowing, etc. All of these elements, including hospital occupancy planning, are very important. During the sarin attack in Tokyo, many people were just rushed off to the hospitals. The hospitals were quickly overwhelmed, though only about 20 percent of these individuals actually suffered from symptoms.

In these kinds of incidents, people may even imagine symptoms. There is an interesting account of the 1997 threat at the B'nai B'rith headquarters in Washington, D.C. Someone left a Petri dish there, on which was written it "yersinia anthracis," a combination of the words for "plague" and for "anthrax." It appeared to be a biological incident. All of the people at the B'nai B'rith headquarters began experiencing symptoms as if it were a chemical attack. So the emergency responders had to deal with this situation and perform decontamination as if it were an actual chemical attack, because of the appearance of all these symptoms, which were of course imagined.

We discussed framing the political issues. Two audiences are involved here: First, there is your constituency to whom you must prove that the government has control of events. Simultaneously, you need to convince the terrorists' backers that they have derived little or no benefit from the attack. Therefore, it is important to think very carefully about terminology used to characterize the incident. A campaign plan is vital, because threats are constant. How should the events be characterized, who is responsible, what are the consequences? Action must be taken to minimize the terrorists' gains. For instance, in the case of the attack on a bus in Jerusalem, which killed many children, Israel should contemplate actions like approaching UNICEF and requesting that resolutions be passed denouncing attacks against children. This type of step will graphically illustrate Israel's point, beyond the words and images at the scene. At times, Israel might want to appeal for assistance, by asking the EU or the US for specific humanitarian aid. Calls for assistance effectively demonstrate that something is happening.

But perhaps the most important consideration should be the "counter-value." For example, in the nuclear dialogue, the talk was about threatening the enemy's population and infrastructure, which would supposedly deter them or induce them to end the war. Obviously, in the case of the people with whom we are dealing, their value system is motivated by different considerations, which require further—in-depth study.

In any event, whatever is done must reinforce the desired political message–that terrorism will not achieve the aims of the terrorist organization.

Tools for Countering Future Terrorism

Eric Herren

Researcher, International Policy Institute for
Counter-Terrorism, Switzerland

What shape do we expect future terrorist activities to take? Most probably it will be a mixture of what we already see around us, enriched with some surprises we are afraid to think about.

This might include assassinations and direct action against governments, together with the more usual pressure on public opinion and psychological warfare. We may see suicide attacks combined with weapons of mass destruction, multiple attacks, and cyber terrorism. Terrorist actors may include known and ad hoc terrorist organisations that have yet to be formed. All of this and many possibilities that we have not yet thought of may be part of future terrorism.

Are we ready to confront this threat ?

I would like focus on existing tools in counter terrorism, and some dilemmas and difficulties in countering terrorism. I would like to provoke some thinking in the direction of additional tools necessary in the fight against terrorism.

It all comes down to the question of the chicken and the egg: What do we do first, kill the crocodiles first or drain the swamp?

The structure of terrorism

Let us take closer look at the ingredients of a terrorist attack. I will concentrate on only few important aspects, taking a "top-down" approach, from the general to the specific. This list can be thought of as a kind of "infrastructure" for a terrorist attack.

Ideological / religious / political movement – Here we find the hotbeds of future terrorist organizations.

Terrorist organization – Included in the terrorist organization are radical supporters, the leadership, the masterminds, economic support activities–both legal and illegal, and all logistic cover operations and institutions. More and more we see organizations networking with other terrorist organizations espousing the same cause.

Strategic planning – Terrorist organizations invest significant efforts in "meta activities," such as public relations, and often use sophisticated tools to steer internal public opinion. Extensive efforts are also directed toward influencing the world audience through psychological warfare. Strategic planning also includes logistics and basic training. Terrorist organizations need to maintain and continually upgrade their arsenals, and to fill the ranks of fighters. Fundraising is another characteristic operation on this level.

Operational activities – In order to be effective, terrorist organizations need to have an intelligence-gathering capability. The use of open sources like the internet aide in target selection. Terrorists also seek to get information by simply monitoring the grey area around private security organisations. The increasing tendency to outsource police and law enforcement tasks to the private sector may also allow terrorists to access information on vulnerabilities.

Tactical preparation – This includes recruiting operatives and planning terrorist attacks. A terror attack is a complex operation. The "shahid," or suicide attacker, is surrounded by several circles of activists who select and arm the human bomb, and send him on his mission. A successful attack is based on intelligence and the processing of real time information, knowledge management, and a certain degree of "dumb luck."

Attack – From the standpoint of the terrorist organizations, an attack is successful if it produces a high body count and maximum destruction, followed by extensive media coverage.

The structure of counter terrorism

Here too, I will touch on only a few of the relevant factors in the counter-terrorism "infrastructure," again, going from the general to the specific. Keep in mind that this list is far from complete.

Public opinion – Terrorism is a kind of psychological warfare; it's aim is to undermine the morale of the targeted nation as well as to influence international public opinion. Thus, counter-terrorism must start at the true frontline–the level of the general public

The media – The media is of crucial importance for both terrorist and counter terrorist strategies.

Political leadership – The leadership of the nation forms the policies and guidelines for counter—terrorist organization and operations.

Think tanks – Interdisciplinary think factories can play a role in advising decision-makers and enhancing counter terrorist strategies.

Intelligence – Intelligence is of central importance in the war against terrorism.

Special operations – Special operations are the spearhead of counter terrorist efforts. They include rescue operations as well as law enforcement, security and military operations.

Counter-terrorism tools

I would like to point out that counter-terrorism begins with a strong and determined counter-terrorism community. In order to effectively fight terrorism, it is necessary to build a community of interest that is single-minded and solutions-oriented. This organization needs an efficient internal communication system; it needs a common language, and a sense of trust and responsibility among members of the community.

Effective counter-terrorism requires the establishment of operational platforms to exchange views, create training scenarios and set up red-teams.

All of the foregoing applies equally to the national and the international levels.

It is also necessary to invest extensive efforts into ensuring that new terrorist organizations don't sprout as quickly as we uproot the ones we now face. In other words, it isn't enough to fight the alligators; we must drain the swamp.

We will now examine the dilemmas and difficulties of each aspect of counter terrorism in relation to the terrorist infrastructure. I will tackle this from the bottom-up, beginning with the more specific and working up to the most general ingredients of counter-terrorism.

Special operations

Special operations are the fundamental activities of counter-terrorism. As an example of the various factors involved, let us take as an example the type of operations that may come into play in the case of a suicide terror attack.

Rescue operations – Once the human bomb is within his chosen target area, special operations will be limited to reducing the impact of the attack. Professional rescue operations will need to take into account that the attack may be a compound one, with secondary attacks planned to target rescue forces. Medical personnel are an integral part of the security plan and play the greatest role in mitigating the effects of the attack.

Security measures – Increased security measures can lead to the discovery of the attacker before he or she can reach the target zone, thus reducing the damage or preventing the attack altogether. Successful security measures include the designation of different security zones ranging from non-target to pre-target and target zones. Each zone is characterized by different security activities, ranging from electronic surveillance to physical barriers.

Defensive activities – This includes special operations against planning and recruiting efforts by specialized cells within the terrorist organizations. Defensive measures must be continually upgraded by constantly re-examining and testing security arrangements. Nothing is more dangerous in security operations than the establishing of routine procedures which lose their sensitivity.

Offensive strikes – Offensive counter-terror operations are special operations directed against the close circle surrounding the suicide bomber–those who recruit the human bombs, equip them with the explosives, instruct them about favourable targets, harbour them before sending them into action and try to cover their tracks. Many nations that strike back at terrorists base such operations on the right to self-defence. The rationale is that the person who "arms and aims" the human bomb is no less culpable than the bomber, and must be held responsible.

Surgical operations – This aspect of counter-terrorism includes counterintelligence activities, as well as special operations against logistics and training infrastructure. Terrorists often hide their activities within legal business or social–even medical or international–organisations. Bomb factories have been found in the same building as nursery schools and hospitals. By the same token, weapons procurement may take place under the legal auspices of a supporting state and fundraising for terrorist organizations may be covered by legal business activities. This type of interaction between terrorist infrastructure and civilian institutions makes special operations against such activities extremely difficult and risky.

Coordinated strategies – Among the most important special operations are those that seek to stem the flow of sympathy and support to terrorist organizations. These operations attempt to knock the wind out of public outrage and hate, the glorification of suicide bombers, and the misleading of young men and women by religious indoctrination. Counter-terrorism at the highest levels must counter disinformation and psychological warfare. Long-term counter-terrorist strategies must include the winning of hearts and minds to successfully win the war against terrorism.

Preventive actions in the virtual world – Lastly, we come to preventive counter-terrorist "street work," carried out by units specifically trained to deal with the "virtual infrastructure" of terrorism. Here, intelligence is derived from the continual monitoring of Internet forums, website, and other forms of digital communications. The goal is to enter the virtual battlefield to pick out potential future terrorists and attempt to open a window for them to integrate back into our society.

Conclusions for Future terrorism

To deal with the threat of future terrorism, we will need to create multinational special operation teams. These teams will include regional intervention units, who will be first on the scene to stabilize the situation and prepare the field for take-over units.

It would be useful to establish an international counter-terrorist unit, which would bring together the best counter-terror solutions from around the world. At the same time, we must establish international and transnational centres of excellence, and create think factories and knowledge-management organizations.

Intelligence

Intelligence is the sense organ of the counter-terrorist organism—the faculty that takes in and processes incoming information. As we did above, we will analyze the components of intelligence using the example of the threat of suicide attacks.

Identification of the threat – Intelligence is the key factor in preventing the attack. Once the potential suicide bomber is identified, security measures can be steered toward a useful end. The time factor here is critical; information processing procedures must work quickly and forward their analysis to the end users at special operations level.

Counterintelligence – Intelligence communities must upgrade their counterintelligence capabilities. Data security is vital to prevent terrorists from gaining access to information that could help in target selection. Intelligence agencies should be able to provide specific recommendations and advise to private institutions at risk of information theft, in order to prevent sensitive information from falling into the hands of terrorists.

Humint / Sigint / Elint – Intelligence gathered from the inner circle of the activists surrounding the "shahid" is based mainly on human sources. The running of such cells is a sensitive and risky business. In many countries, human Intelligence is very much a neglected art form. Too many efforts have been, and are being, invested in other means of intelligence gathering. We must come back to the human sources within our own organizations, including police and customs officers and other government employees. The police officer on his own beat must be successfully integrated into the information-gathering process; he has intimate knowledge of his own area, and will be the first to know of any unusual activity.

Unfortunately the flow of information is often blocked by obstacles within the system. Even as we collect the best resources from our peripheries and bring them together in federal institutions, we may be missing some of the best resources that are already available in our midst.

Psy Ops – Psychological operations involving the intelligence community should be directed not only against the public relation efforts of the terrorist organization, but should also aim to disrupt the flow of communications within the different levels of the terrorist organizations. This kind of activity can help to keep the terrorist organizations busy preserving their own structures, and may lead to mistakes on their part.

Multinational intelligence community – Intelligence aimed at terrorist organizations and their strategic efforts includes humint, sigint, and elint. The most important factor in this kind of activity is international cooperation. Often this part of the game is played on the international stage far from the "hot spots" and well protected from unwanted attention. Examples are operations to prevent terrorist fundraising and weapons procurement.

Thermostat – Intelligence agencies need to establish sensors within ideological, religious, and political movements in order to gauge the "temperature" of the more radical elements and take preventive measures where necessary. Difficulties in the struggle against terrorist organizations often include the lack of cooperation between all the agencies involved. While healthy competition is part of the game on the national, as well as the international level, it is clear that success in the war against terrorism is only reached through partnership and trust. Intelligence agencies are notorious for spreading their efforts far and wide. In order to avoid this, the intelligence community should be gathered under a common umbrella, coordinated, and guided by political decisions.

Needless to say, intelligence is crucial to the success of special operations of all kinds. But more than this, it is the job of intelligence to create a round table for the exchange of views. Intelligence agencies should strive as far as possible to achieve an interdisciplinary approach.

I would like to highlight an issue common within intelligence communities: the need to determine the end-user for the agency's products. All too often, intelligence is collected merely to support old institutions and infrastructures within the intelligence agency. It is vitally important that intelligence reach political decision-makers so that it can become part of their consultancy tools.

There is also the issue of how to deal with the media. In many countries, the relation between intelligence and media are like cat-and-mouse, with the "right to know" and censorship producing a good deal of friction. Public opinion and intelligence are sometimes strange bedfellows; in times of threat, the public calls for visible results from the agencies. Here the dilemma is to explain what is being done without jeopardizing the success of intelligence operations.

Conclusions for Future terrorism

The threat of future terrorism will force the intelligence community to establish multinational intelligence databases, with reasonable access for partner states. This will naturally lead to the dilemma of protecting the sources of the intelligence and establishing who gets access, and how much access. One simple rule could be: the more a state gives, the greater its access.

It will also be necessary to upgrade our ability to successfully process information under time pressure. It makes no sense to become a vacuum cleaner, sucking in all kinds of information, if the means of analyzing and interpreting this information are lacking. Analyzed information must be able to flow back to the end users and other elements of the counter terrorist community:

Here we will need to learn about and integrate better knowledge management processes. Do we fully recognize the power of open sources? We will need specialists to analyze open sources in all languages and in every open forum.

Human intelligence will be the main resource for effective intelligence gathering. The human factor must become our main concern. Intelligence officers will need purposeful career planning and feedback for successful activities. To be proud of his or her job is one of the main sources of motivation in a career that has little open reward or glory.

Think tanks

One of the most neglected of counter-terrorist tools is the think tank. Academic "think factories" are helpful in providing a broader view of the phenomena of terrorism. They are removed from the actual stage of combat and are able to focus on the problem from all possible angles and positions.

Think tanks should deal with the actual threats, in addition to learning from the overall history of terrorism. Their task should include attempting to foresee the future and "think the unthinkable."

Members of think tanks should include former and present members of the counter-terrorism community, as well as those who can contribute to the vision. Think tanks should become consultants and critical observers supplying feedback to the counter-terrorism community, and providing forecasts and partnership in solution-oriented task forces. We will also have to learn to accept them as teachers and instructors.

Conclusions for Future terrorism

What is needed is a successful networking of think tanks. These organizations are probably the only ones that can keep up with the pace of terrorist networking. Official governmental operations and coordinated strategies are often held back by office procedures, unnecessary bureaucracy, and political interests.

Think tanks create the possibility of online brainstorming forums, bringing together huge resources of intellectual potential–a kind of creative solution-seeking that can be extremely helpful.

We will need interdisciplinary institutions whose activities are devoted to finding global strategies and are willing be part of a whole. We need international centers of competence, which will concentrate on specialized tasks as an interdisciplinary contribution to the fight against terror. An example is the recently established Center for the Study of Militant Islam.

Regarding future terrorist threats–it is likely enough that science fiction will become a relevant part of mental preparedness for future terrorism.

Politics

Politics and counter-terrorism are at the head of virtually every national agenda today. Let me just point out several key issues with regard to successful measures against terrorism.

Political will – Political commitment to combat terrorism is the fundamental motivator behind all counter-terrorist activities. The will to fight terrorism–and especially to deal with the grey zones where terrorism and organized crime meet–are crucial for political decision-makers. But let us not be dreamers; today in many countries the grey zones are an integral part of the economic infrastructure of the nation. It will be hard to get countries to cut off funding to terrorists when this funding is seen as a legitimate part of the national economy.

Leadership – National and international leadership in the war against terrorism is necessary in order to concentrate the efforts of all relevant sources.

Definitions – An international definition of terrorism if crucial and fundamental. Such a definition will serve as a basis for counter-terrorist activities, and an operational tool to expand our ability to combat terrorism on the international level. Too many groups that employ terrorism still hide behind the facade of "freedom fighters" and "insurgents."

Laws – Based on the political will of the leaders, and supported by international definitions, nations must create and change their laws to be better prepared to meet the emerging threat of terrorism and organized crime.

Clear political decisions – We must demand that political leaders make difficult decisions; in the absence of political guidance, counter-terrorism organizations all too often become institutions for managing problems rather than solving them. Politics is an important partner in counter-terrorism, and is responsible for controlling and supporting counter-terrorism tools.

Politicians must impress not only public opinion by their determination to fight terrorism, but also must send clear signals to extremist groups. We further expect from politics a professional handling of the media.

Conclusions for Future terrorism

The fight against future terrorism will demand political courage, as well as perseverance, in order to mitigate the impact of future attacks. Future terrorism will also entail great political flexibility and the need to adapt. We will need political vision. Most of all, our leaders will need the ability to absorb and integrate reality into their decision-making process.

Media

Most of the public's knowledge of terrorism comes from the media. Many international news outlets concentrate only on the most obvious stage of terrorist activities–the attack itself. In fact, the media is often the first responder to a terrorist attack.

Using the example of a suicide attack, the media will home in on the scene of the attack, broadcasting images of the death and destruction. These pictures are the strongest weapon in the hands of terrorist organizations; they show results to the targeted population and play to an international audience. These images also prove the success of the operation to the terrorists' constituency, while at the same time satisfying their sick motivation to kill innocents.

But where is the media's interest in backstage terrorist activities? Such activity is the real "bread and butter" of terrorism, and deserves at least as much coverage as do terror attacks. However, this kind of coverage requires intensive investment, professionalism and journalistic expertise, and the success of such TV documentaries is not guaranteed.

Many media agencies use the term of "Info-tainment" to describe their broadcasts. The average audience wants to know who is the bad guy and who is the good guy without investing too much thought. Information must be cut into small, bit-sized pieces that can easily be swallowed with no stomach-ache.

Modern terrorists try to influence decision-makers through public opinion. This kind of psychological warfare is often supported by the media by the lack of professionalism of on-scene journalists, who themselves become part of the action and loose their sense of objectivity. The terrorists' message is transmitted through the good offices of the international media. The effects of this reportage could be mitigated by paying the same attention to backstage terrorist activities.

Conclusions for Future terrorism

It is in our interests to educate the media to their responsibilities as a first responder to terrorist attacks. Media can be used and/or misused as part of psychological operations. The media can become a partner in counter-terrorism if we cooperate and if we strictly draw the borders between responsible journalism and playing into the hands of terrorists.

Future terrorism may well include "media terrorism"–information channels could be hijacked and panic spread by pre-prepared images, and fake political statements. This too, is something for which we need to be prepared.

Public opinion

Terrorist attacks target public opinion in several ways. First: a successful attack aims to lower the morale and weaken the resistance of the targeted population. The terrorists' goal is to create a feeling of general vulnerability among the citizens. This psychological warfare results in enormous pressure on the government to take action (or over-reaction), which results in international condemnation of the targeted nation.

Secondly, the attack is also used by terrorist organizations to spread their message to the whole world. Unlike the old forms of terrorism, which sometimes had very clear political messages, today's terrorist strategy is twofold: it sends shockwaves through the civilized world; and it uses its "successes" to call for sympathizers to join the jihad. Each successful attack is another page written in the terrorist handbook used to teach the next generation of extremists.

Public Education – A successful counter-terrorist strategy must include a powerful effort to educate and teach citizens about the dangers of terrorist manipulation and the impact of psychological warfare.

Security measures – Increased security measures can only be implemented if public opinion supports these actions. It is the general population that suffers from security checks and the loss of privacy. Therefore, much more attention should be directed to this most vital part of counter-terrorist strategy–with an emphasis on education. Terrorism attacks the public morale and the emotional balance of each individual. We must do all we can to strengthen this most important partner in counter-terrorism.

Conclusions for Future terrorism

Public support is critical for any long-term counter-terrorist strategy. To paraphrase Dr. Ganor: "Counter-terrorist forces can win the battle but lose the war, if citizens are afraid to use public transportation or to go to public place."